Investment Banking
Focus Notes

JOSHUA ROSENBAUM
JOSHUA PEARL

Contents

About the Authors

JOSHUA ROSENBAUM is a Managing Director at UBS Investment Bank in the Global Industrial Group. He originates, structures, and advises on M&A, corporate finance, and capital markets transactions. Previously, he worked at the International Finance Corporation, the direct investment division of the World Bank. He received his AB from Harvard and his MBA with Baker Scholar honors from Harvard Business School.

JOSHUA PEARL is an investment analyst at Brahman Capital Corp. Previously, he structured and executed leveraged loan and high yield bond financings, as well as leveraged buyouts and restructurings as a Director at UBS Investment Bank in Leveraged Finance. Prior to UBS, he worked at Moelis & Company and Deutsche Bank. He received his BS in Business from Indiana University's Kelley School of Business.

CONTACT THE AUTHORS

Please feel free to contact JOSHUA ROSENBAUM and JOSHUA PEARL with any questions, comments, or suggestions for future editions at josh@investmentbankingbook.com.

Introduction

Investment Banking: FOCUS NOTES provides a comprehensive, yet streamlined, review of the basic skills and concepts discussed in *Investment Banking: Valuation, Leveraged Buyouts, and Mergers & Acquisitions, Second Edition.* The focus notes are designed for use both as a companion to the main book, as well as on a standalone basis. The *Investment Banking* suite of products, including the primary hardcover text, valuation models, workbook and focus notes, is centered on the primary valuation methodologies currently used on Wall Street—namely, comparable companies analysis, precedent transactions analysis, discounted cash flow (DCF) analysis, and leveraged buyout (LBO) analysis—as well as detailed mergers & acquisitions (M&A) analysis from both a sell-side and buy-side perspective.

FOCUS NOTES seek to help solidify knowledge of these core financial topics as true mastery must be tested, honed, and retested over time. It is the ultimate self-help tool for students, job seekers, and existing finance professionals, as well as in formal classroom and training settings.

FOCUS NOTES is designed to optimize mastering the critical financial tools discussed in *Investment Banking, Second Edition* and therefore corresponds to its chapters, as shown below:

- Chapter 1: Comparable Companies Analysis
- Chapter 2: Precedent Transactions Analysis
- Chapter 3: Discounted Cash Flow Analysis
- Chapter 4: Leveraged Buyouts
- Chapter 5: LBO Analysis
- Chapter 6: Sell-Side M&A
- Chapter 7: Buy-Side M&A

Chapter 1
Comparable Companies Analysis

Comparable Companies Analysis Steps

Step I.   Select the Universe of Comparable Companies
Step II. Locate the Necessary Financial Information
Step III. Spread Key Statistics, Ratios, and Trading Multiples
Step IV. Benchmark the Comparable Companies
Step V.   Determine Valuation

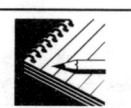

Overview of Comparable Companies Analysis

- Provides a market benchmark against which a banker can establish valuation for private company or analyze the value of public company at given point in time
- Built upon premise that similar companies provide highly relevant reference point for valuing a target company
  - Share key business and financial characteristics, performance drivers, and risks
  - Valuation parameters can be established for the target by determining relative positioning among peers
- Broad range of applications, most notably for various M&A situations, IPOs, restructurings, and investment decisions
- Selecting universe of comparable companies for target is core of analysis
  - Peers are benchmarked against each another and the target based on various financial statistics and ratios
  - Valuation multiples utilize a measure of value in numerator and operating metric in denominator
- Designed to reflect "current" valuation based on prevailing market conditions and sentiment
  - Market trading levels may be subject to periods of irrational investor sentiment that skew valuation either too high or too low
  - No two companies are exactly the same
  - May fail to accurately capture a given company's true value

Step I: Select the Universe of Comparable Companies

Study the Target

- Process of learning the in-depth "story" of target should be exhaustive
- Read and study as much company- and sector-specific material as possible

Public Targets

- Annual (10-K) and quarterly (10-Q) SEC filings
- Consensus research estimates
- Equity and fixed income research reports
- Press releases, earnings call transcripts, investor presentations, and corporate websites

Private Targets

- Greater challenge to locate information (unless company has public debt)
- Corporate websites, sector research reports, news runs, and trade journals
- Public competitors' SEC filings, research reports, and investor presentations
- Banker is provided with detailed business and financial information in organized M&A sale process

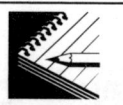

Step I: Select the Universe of Comparable Companies

Identify Key Characteristics of the Target for Comparison Purposes

Business and Financial Profile Framework

Business Profile	Financial Profile
▪ Sector	▪ Size
▪ Products and Services	▪ Profitability
▪ Customers and End Markets	▪ Growth Profile
▪ Distribution Channels	▪ Return on Investment
▪ Geography	▪ Credit Profile

Step I: Select the Universe of Comparable Companies

Screen for Comparable Companies

- Begin screen after target's basic business and financial characteristics are researched and understood
- Examination of target's public competitors is usually best place to begin
- Competitors share key business and financial characteristics and are susceptible to similar opportunities and risks
  - Focus on identifying companies with similar business profile
  - More detailed financial benchmarking is performed in Step IV
- Sources
  - 10-Ks, annual proxy statement, investor presentations, and credit rating agencies reports (e.g., Moody's, S&P, and Fitch)
  - Equity research reports, especially initiating coverage reports
  - Excerpts from fairness opinion contained in proxy statement for recent M&A transaction
  - Bloomberg Industry Classification Standard ("BICS") codes
- Potential to tier selected companies by size, business focus, or geography
- Difficult to locate "pure" comparable companies
- Often as much "art" as "science"

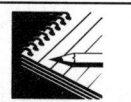

Step II: Locate the Necessary Financial Information

- Valuation is driven on basis of both historical performance (e.g., last twelve months (LTM) financial data) and expected future performance (e.g., consensus estimates for future calendar years)
- SEC Filings – Historical Financials
  - Used as source for historical financial information (both annual and LTM), balance sheet data, basic shares outstanding, stock options/warrants data, and information on non-recurring items
  - 10-K (Annual Report) – annual audited report, provides comprehensive overview of company and prior year performance
  - 10-Q (Quarterly Report) – quarterly unaudited report, provides overview of most recent quarter and year-to-date (YTD) period
  - 8-K (Current Report) – reports occurrence of *material* corporate events or changes ("triggering event")
  - Proxy Statement – contains material information regarding matters shareholders are expected to vote on
- Equity Research – Estimates
  - Research reports – provide individual analyst estimates of future company performance and include estimates of sales, EBITDA and/or EBIT, and EPS for future quarters and future two- or three-year period
  - Initiating coverage research reports are more comprehensive
  - Consensus estimates (e.g., Bloomberg) are used as basis for calculating forward-looking trading multiples in trading comps

- Press Releases and News Runs
  - News of earnings announcements, declaration of dividends, management changes, and M&A and capital markets transactions
- Financial Information Services (e.g., Bloomberg)
  - Key source for obtaining SEC filings, research reports, consensus estimates, and press releases

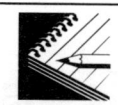

Step III: Spread Key Statistics, Ratios, and Trading Multiples

- Once the necessary financial information for each of the comparables has been located, it is entered into an input page.
- The input page data, in turn, feeds into output sheets that are used to benchmark the comparables.

Input Sheet	Output Sheets
<ul><li>Enter a company's financial data into an input page</li><li>Feeds into summary output sheets used to benchmark the comparables</li><li>Designed to assist in calculating the key financial statistics, ratios, and multiples for the comparables universe</li></ul>	<ul><li>Summary of key financial data for each comparable company</li><li>Data is presented in clear and succinct format for easy comparison</li><li>Serves as basis for identifying, analyzing and comparing comparable companies</li></ul>

Step III: Spread Key Statistics, Ratios, and Trading Multiples

Calculation of Key Financial Statistics and Ratios

Size	■ Market Valuation: equity value and enterprise value ■ Key Financial Data: sales, gross profit, EBITDA, EBIT, and net income
Profitability	■ Gross profit, EBITDA, EBIT, and net income margins
Growth Profile	■ Historical and estimated growth rates
Return on Investment	■ ROIC, ROE, ROA, and dividend yield
Credit Profile	■ Leverage ratios, coverage ratios, and credit ratings

Step III: Spread Key Statistics, Ratios, and Trading Multiples

Size: Market Valuation

- Equity Value ("market capitalization")
    - Value represented by company's basic shares outstanding plus "in-the-money" stock options, warrants, and convertible securities—collectively, "fully diluted shares outstanding"
    - Calculated by multiplying company's current share price by fully diluted shares outstanding

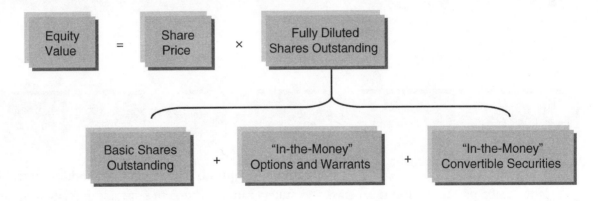

Step III: Spread Key Statistics, Ratios, and Trading Multiples

Size: Market Valuation (continued)

- Enterprise Value ("total enterprise value" or "firm value")
  - Sum of all ownership interests in company and claims on assets from both debt and equity holders
  - Equity value component is calculated on fully diluted basis

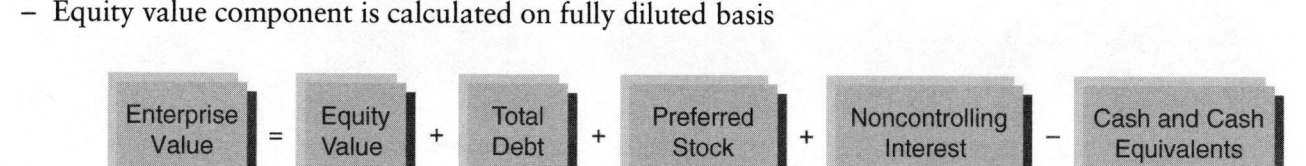

Enterprise Value = Equity Value + Total Debt + Preferred Stock + Noncontrolling Interest − Cash and Cash Equivalents

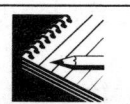

Step III: Spread Key Statistics, Ratios, and Trading Multiples

Size: Key Financial Data

Sales

- First line item, or "top line," on income statement
- Represents total dollar amount realized by company through sale of products and services
- Sales levels and trends are key factor in determining company's relative positioning among peer

Gross Profit

- Profit earned by company after subtracting costs directly related to production of products and services (COGS)
- Key indicator of operational efficiency and pricing power
- Usually expressed as percentage of sales

EBITDA

- Earnings Before Interest, Taxes, Depreciation and Amortization
- Non-GAAP financial measure
- Calculated by taking operating income and adding back depreciation and amortization
- Widely-used proxy for operating cash flow
- Independent of capital structure (i.e., interest expense) and tax regime (i.e., tax expense)

Step III: Spread Key Statistics, Ratios, and Trading Multiples

Size: Key Financial Data (continued)

EBIT

- <u>E</u>arnings <u>B</u>efore <u>I</u>nterest and <u>T</u>axes
- Reported as operating income, operating profit, or income from operations
- Independent of capital structure (i.e., interest expense) and tax regime (i.e., tax expense)

Net Income

- Residual profit after company's expenses have been netted out
- Wall Street views net income on a per share basis (i.e., EPS)

Step III: Spread Key Statistics, Ratios, and Trading Multiples

Growth Profile

- Historical and estimated future growth rates
- Compound annual growth rates (CAGRs)
- Historical EPS must be adjusted for non-recurring items

Historical and Estimated Diluted EPS Growth Rates

	Fiscal Year Ending December 31,						
	2009A	2010A	2011A	CAGR ('09 - '11)	2012E	2013E	CAGR ('11 - '13)
Diluted Earnings Per Share	$1.00	$1.15	$1.30	14.0%	$1.50	$1.65	12.7%
% growth		15.0%	13.0%		15.4%	10.0%	
Long-term growth rate							12.0%

= (Ending Value / Beginning Value) ^ (1 / Ending Year - Beginning Year) - 1
= ($1.30 / $1.00) ^ (1 / (2011 - 2009)) - 1

Source: Consensus Estimates

Step III: Spread Key Statistics, Ratios, and Trading Multiples

Profitability

- Gross Profit Margin – measures percentage of sales remaining after subtracting COGS
  - Driven by company's direct cost per unit, such as materials, manufacturing, and direct labor involved in production

$$\text{Gross Profit Margin} = \frac{\text{Gross Profit (Sales – COGS)}}{\text{Sales}}$$

- EBITDA and EBIT margin – accepted standards for measuring company's operating profitability
  - Independent of capital structure (i.e., interest expense) and tax regime (i.e., tax expense)

$$\text{EBITDA Margin} = \frac{\text{EBITDA}}{\text{Sales}} \qquad \text{EBIT Margin} = \frac{\text{EBIT}}{\text{Sales}}$$

Profitability (continued)

- Net Income Margin – measures company's overall profitability as opposed to operating profitability
  - Impacted by capital structure and tax regime

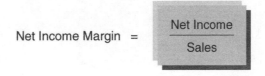

$$\text{Net Income Margin} = \frac{\text{Net Income}}{\text{Sales}}$$

Step III: Spread Key Statistics, Ratios, and Trading Multiples

Return on Investment

- Return on Invested Capital (ROIC) – measures return generated by all capital provided to company

$$ROIC = \frac{EBIT}{\text{Average Net Debt + Equity}}$$

- Return on Equity (ROE) – measures return generated on equity provided to company by shareholders

$$ROE = \frac{\text{Net Income}}{\text{Average Shareholders' Equity}}$$

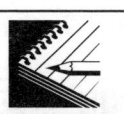

Step III: Spread Key Statistics, Ratios, and Trading Multiples

Return on Investment (continued)

- Return on Assets (ROA) – measures return generated by company's asset base

$$ROA = \frac{\text{Net Income}}{\text{Average Total Assets}}$$

- Dividend Yield – measures annual dividends per share paid by company to shareholders

$$\text{Implied Dividend Yield} = \frac{\text{Most Recent Quarterly Dividend Per Share} \times 4}{\text{Current Share Price}}$$

Step III: Spread Key Statistics, Ratios, and Trading Multiples

Credit Profile

- Leverage – refers to company's debt level
    - Reveals great deal about company's financial policy, risk profile, and capacity for growth
    - Debt-to-EBITDA

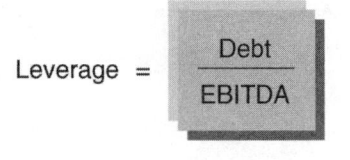

$$\text{Leverage} = \frac{\text{Debt}}{\text{EBITDA}}$$

- Debt-to-total capitalization

$$\text{Debt-to-Total Capitalization} = \frac{\text{Debt}}{\text{Debt + Preferred Stock + Noncontrolling Interest + Equity}}$$

Step III: Spread Key Statistics, Ratios, and Trading Multiples

Credit Profile (continued)

- Coverage – company's ability to meet ("cover") interest expense obligations
  - Variations include EBITDA-to-interest expense, (EBITDA less capex)-to-interest expense, and EBIT-to-interest expense

$$\text{Interest Coverage Ratio} = \frac{\text{EBITDA, (EBITDA} - \text{Capex), or EBIT}}{\text{Interest Expense}}$$

- Credit Ratings
  - Measures a company's ability to make full and timely payments of amounts due on debt obligations
  - Typically required for companies seeking to raise debt financing in capital markets

Step III: Spread Key Statistics, Ratios, and Trading Multiples

	Moody's	S&P	Fitch	Definition
Investment Grade	Aaa	AAA	AAA	Highest Quality
	Aa1	AA+	AA+	
	Aa2	AA	AA	Very High Quality
	Aa3	AA-	AA–	
	A1	A+	A+	
	A2	A	A	High Quality
	A3	A–	A–	
	Baa1	BBB+	BBB+	
	Baa2	BBB	BBB	Medium Grade
	Baa3	BBB-	BBB–	
Non-Investment Grade	Ba1	BB+	BB+	
	Ba2	BB	BB	Speculative
	Ba3	BB–	BB–	
	B1	B+	B+	
	B2	B	B	Highly Speculative
	B3	B–	B–	
	Caa1	CCC+	CCC+	
	Caa2	CCC	CCC	Substantial Risk
	Caa3	CCC-	CCC–	
	Ca	CC	CC	
	C	C	C	Extremely Speculative /
	–	D	D	Default

Step III: Spread Key Statistics, Ratios, and Trading Multiples

Supplemental Financial Concepts and Calculations

- Calculation of LTM Financial Data
  - Financial results for previous four quarters are summed to measure financial performance for most recent annual or LTM period
  - Financial information is sourced from company's most recent 10-K, 10-Q, and earnings press release in an 8-K
  - No LTM calculations are necessary in event most recent quarter is fourth quarter of company's fiscal year

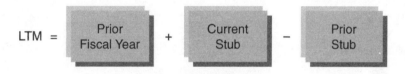

LTM = Prior Fiscal Year + Current Stub − Prior Stub

Step III: Spread Key Statistics, Ratios, and Trading Multiples

Supplemental Financial Concepts and Calculations (continued)

- Calendarization of Financial Data
  - Majority of U.S. public filers report financial performance in accordance with fiscal year (FY) ending 12/31
  - Some companies report on different schedule (e.g., fiscal year ending 4/30)
  - Any variation in fiscal year ends among comparable companies must be addressed for benchmarking purposes
  - Calendarization adjusts each company's financials to conform to single calendar year end

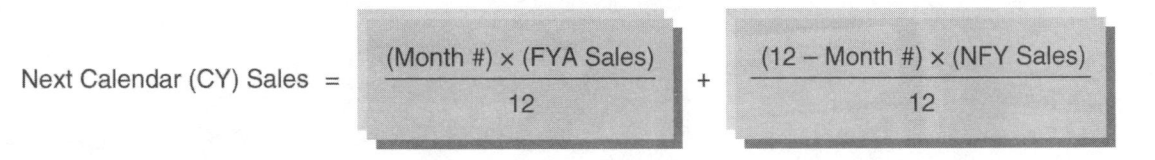

$$\text{Next Calendar (CY) Sales} = \frac{(\text{Month \#}) \times (\text{FYA Sales})}{12} + \frac{(12 - \text{Month \#}) \times (\text{NFY Sales})}{12}$$

- Adjustments for Non-Recurring Items
  - Standard practice to adjust reported financial data for non-recurring items
  - Failure to do so may lead to calculation of misleading ratios and multiples
  - Involves add-back or elimination of one-time charges and gains
  - Important to distinguish between pre-tax and after-tax amounts
- Adjustments for Recent Events
  - Must also make adjustments for recent events (e.g., M&A transactions, financing activities, stock splits)

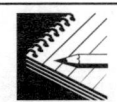

Step III: Spread Key Statistics, Ratios, and Trading Multiples

Calculation of Key Trading Multiples

- Equity Value Multiples
  - Denominator must be financial statistic that flows <u>only</u> to equity holders, such as net income (or diluted EPS)
  - Price-to-Earnings Ratio / Equity Value-to-Net Income Multiple
    - Most widely recognized trading multiple
    - Can be viewed as measure of how much investors are willing to pay for a dollar of company's current or future earnings
    - Impacted by capital structure and tax regime

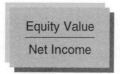

- Enterprise Value Multiples
  - Denominator employs a financial statistic that flows to <u>both</u> debt and equity holders

Step III: Spread Key Statistics, Ratios, and Trading Multiples

Calculation of Key Trading Multiples (continued)

- Enterprise Value-to-EBITDA and Enterprise Value-to-EBIT Multiples
  - Serves as valuation standard for most sectors
  - Independent of capital structure and taxes
  - EV/EBIT is less commonly used than EV/EBITDA due to differences in D&A among companies

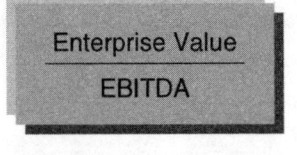

$$\frac{\text{Enterprise Value}}{\text{EBITDA}}$$

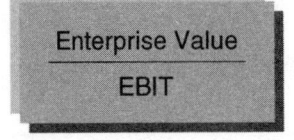

$$\frac{\text{Enterprise Value}}{\text{EBIT}}$$

- Enterprise Value-to-Sales Multiple
  - Relevant for companies with little or no earnings
  - Typically less pertinent than other multiples
  - Sanity check on earnings-based multiples

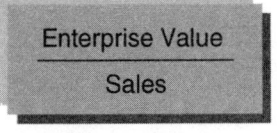

$$\frac{\text{Enterprise Value}}{\text{Sales}}$$

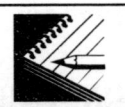

Step IV: Benchmark the Comparable Companies

- Centers on analyzing and comparing each of the comparable companies with one another and target
- Objective is to determine the target's relative ranking to frame valuation accordingly
  - Hone in on selected group of closest comparables as basis for establishing target's implied valuation range
  - Closest comparables are generally those most similar to target in terms of business and financial profile
- Two-step process
  - Benchmark key financial statistics and ratios for target and comparables in order to establish relative positioning
  - Analyze and compare trading multiples for peer group

Step IV: Benchmark the Comparable Companies

Benchmark the Financial Statistics and Ratios

- Comparison of target and comparables universe on basis of key financial performance metrics
- Include measures of size, profitability, growth, returns, and credit strength
  - Core value drivers
  - Typically translate directly into relative valuation
- Establish relative positioning
  - Focus on identifying closest or "best" comparables and noting potential outliers
- Benchmarking analysis goes beyond quantitative comparison of comparables' financial metrics
  - Need to have strong understanding of each comparable company's "story" to truly assess target's relative strength

Benchmark the Trading Multiples

- Assess relative valuation for each of the comparable companies
- Certain outliers may need to be excluded or comparables may be further tiered (e.g., on the basis of size, sub-sector, or ranging from closest to peripheral)
- Trading multiples for best comparables are noted
  - Assigned greater emphasis for framing valuation

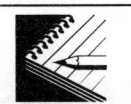

Step IV: Benchmark the Comparable Companies

ValueCo Corporation
Benchmarking Analysis – Financial Statistics and Ratios, Page 1
($ in millions, except per share data)

Company	Ticker	Market Valuation Equity Value	Market Valuation Enterprise Value	LTM Financial Statistics Sales	LTM Financial Statistics Gross Profit	LTM Financial Statistics EBITDA	LTM Financial Statistics EBIT	LTM Financial Statistics Net Income	LTM Profitability Margins Gross Profit (%)	LTM Profitability Margins EBITDA (%)	LTM Profitability Margins EBIT (%)	LTM Profitability Margins Net Income (%)	Growth Rates Sales Hist. 1-year	Growth Rates Sales Est. 1-year	Growth Rates EBITDA Hist. 1-year	Growth Rates EBITDA Est. 1-year	Growth Rates EPS Hist. 1-year	Growth Rates EPS Est. 1-year	Growth Rates EPS Est. LT
ValueCo Corporation	NA	-	-	$3,385	$1,155	$700	$500	$248	34%	21%	15%	7%	10%	9%	15%	9%	NA	NA	NA
Tier I: Specialty Chemicals																			
BuyerCo	BUY	$9,800	$11,600	$8,560	$2,329	$1,443	$1,279	$705	36%	22%	20%	11%	14%	8%	22%	8%	27%	10%	7%
Sherman Co.	SHR	5,600	8,101	5,895	1,411	1,047	752	419	33%	18%	13%	7%	10%	7%	10%	7%	11%	11%	9%
Pearl Corp.	PRL	5,172	5,856	4,284	1,585	839	625	325	37%	20%	15%	8%	10%	7%	10%	7%	10%	15%	11%
Gasparro Corp.	JDG	5,000	6,750	4,725	1,680	900	725	388	36%	19%	15%	8%	8%	11%	5%	15%	6%	31%	12%
Kumra Inc.	KUM	4,852	5,345	3,187	922	665	506	248	29%	21%	16%	8%	10%	8%	10%	8%	11%	20%	10%
Mean									34%	20%	16%	8%	10%	8%	11%	9%	13%	17%	10%
Median									36%	20%	15%	8%	10%	8%	10%	8%	11%	15%	10%
Tier II: Commodity / Diversified Chemicals																			
Falloon Group	FLN	$7,480	$11,254	$11,835	$3,373	$1,636	$1,044	$465	29%	14%	9%	4%	5%	4%	5%	4%	5%	18%	5%
Goodson Corp.	GDS	4,160	5,660	4,769	1,431	763	525	214	30%	16%	11%	4%	10%	5%	10%	5%	17%	16%	9%
Pryor Industries	PRI	3,926	4,166	3,682	1,178	569	421	227	32%	15%	11%	6%	5%	5%	5%	5%	2%	11%	10%
Lanzarone Global	LNZ	3,230	3,823	3,712	854	578	430	233	23%	16%	12%	6%	5%	4%	5%	4%	4%	16%	8%
McMenamin & Co.	MCM	3,193	3,193	3,223	903	355	226	119	28%	11%	7%	4%	5%	15%	5%	15%	7%	20%	12%
Mean									28%	14%	10%	5%	6%	7%	6%	7%	7%	16%	9%
Median									29%	15%	11%	4%	5%	5%	5%	5%	5%	16%	9%
Tier III: Small-Cap Chemicals																			
S. Momper & Co.	MOMP	$2,240	$2,921	$2,077	$457	$378	$295	$130	22%	18%	14%	6%	5%	11%	5%	11%	7%	8%	5%
Adler Worldwide	ADL	1,217	1,463	1,550	387	245	183	89	25%	16%	12%	6%	5%	5%	5%	5%	7%	8%	7%
Schachter & Sons	STM	1,125	1,674	1,703	426	238	170	76	25%	14%	10%	4%	11%	15%	11%	15%	16%	19%	11%
Girshin Holdings	MGP	1,035	1,298	1,606	273	177	112	52	17%	11%	7%	3%	5%	15%	5%	15%	12%	15%	8%
Crespin International	MCR	872	1,222	1,443	390	190	133	61	27%	13%	9%	4%	5%	15%	4%	14%	5%	10%	6%
Mean									23%	14%	10%	5%	6%	12%	6%	12%	10%	12%	7%
Median									25%	14%	10%	4%	5%	15%	5%	14%	7%	10%	7%
Overall																			
Mean									29%	16%	12%	6%	8%	9%	8%	9%	10%	15%	9%
Median									29%	16%	12%	6%	5%	8%	5%	7%	15%	9%
High									37%	22%	20%	11%	14%	15%	22%	15%	27%	31%	12%
Low									17%	11%	7%	3%	5%	4%	4%	4%	2%	8%	5%

Source: Company filings, Bloomberg, Consensus Estimates
Note: Last twelve months data based on September 30, 2012. Estimated annual financial data based on a calendar year.

Step IV: Benchmark the Comparable Companies

ValueCo Corporation
Benchmarking Analysis – Financial Statistics and Ratios, Page 2
($ in millions, except per share data)

Company	Ticker	FYE	General Predicted Beta	ROIC (%)	ROE (%)	ROA (%)	Implied Div. Yield (%)	Debt / Tot. Cap. (%)	Debt / EBITDA (x)	Net Debt / EBITDA (x)	EBITDA / Int. Exp. (x)	EBITDA - Cpx / Int. (x)	EBIT / Int. Exp. (x)	Moody's	S&P
					Return on Investment			LTM Leverage Ratios			LTM Coverage Ratios			Credit Ratings	
ValueCo Corporation	NA	Dec-31	NA	10%	7%	4%	NA	30%	2.1x	1.9x	7.0x	5.5x	5.0x	NA	NA
Tier I: Specialty Chemicals															
Buyer Co	BUY	Dec-31	1.24	30%	29%	9%	0%	47%	1.5x	1.2x	10.1x	8.8x	9.0x	Ba2	BB
Sherman Co.	SHR	Dec-31	1.35	16%	18%	6%	2%	57%	3.0x	2.4x	13.8x	10.7x	9.9x	Baa2	BBB
Pearl Corp.	PRL	Dec-31	1.58	19%	14%	7%	0%	37%	1.8x	0.8x	18.4x	7.1x	6.2x	Baa3	BBB-
Gasparro Corp.	JDG	Dec-31	1.25	21%	23%	8%	2%	52%	2.1x	1.9x	9.0x	7.0x	7.3x	Baa3	BBB-
Kumra Inc.	KUM	Dec-31	1.50	17%	10%	6%	2%	25%	1.3x	0.8x	11.0x	8.7x	8.4x	Baa1	BBB+
Mean			1.38	21%	19%	7%	1%	44%	1.9x	1.4x	10.5x	8.4x	8.2x		
Median			1.35	19%	18%	7%	2%	47%	1.8x	1.2x	10.1x	8.7x	8.4x		
Tier II: Commodity / Diversified Chemicals															
Falloon Group	FLN	Dec-31	1.69	16%	14%	4%	3%	55%	2.5x	2.2x	5.7x	3.8x	3.6x	Ba3	BB
Goodson Corp.	GDS	Dec-31	1.45	15%	11%	5%	1%	52%	2.9x	2.0x	4.2x	3.0x	2.9x	Baa1	BBB-
Pryor, Industries	PRI	Dec-31	1.46	14%	8%	5%	1%	19%	1.1x	0.4x	11.1x	8.9x	8.2x	Baa2	BBB
Lanzarone Global	LNZ	Dec-31	1.68	17%	12%	6%	0%	27%	1.3x	1.0x	10.7x	7.9x	7.9x	Ba3	BB-
McMenamin & Co.	MCM	Dec-31	1.64	12%	7%	4%	1%	18%	1.2x	0.0x	10.6x	8.2x	6.7x	Ba2	BB-
Mean			1.58	15%	10%	5%	1%	34%	1.8x	1.1x	8.5x	6.4x	5.9x		
Median			1.64	15%	11%	5%	1%	27%	1.3x	0.1x	10.6x	7.9x	6.7x		
Tier III: Small-Cap Chemicals															
S. Mompor & Co.	MOMP	Dec-31	1.14	15%	9%	6%	4%	40%	2.6x	1.8x	4.5x	3.7x	3.5x	Ba1	BB
Adler Worldwide	ADL	Dec-31	1.46	12%	7%	3%	4%	22%	1.6x	1.0x	6.2x	5.0x	4.7x	Ba2	BB
Schacter & Sons	STM	Dec-31	1.90	12%	8%	3%	1%	38%	2.5x	2.3x	5.0x	3.2x	3.6x	Ba3	BB-
Girshin Holdings	MGP	Dec-31	1.55	13%	9%	4%	3%	34%	1.8x	1.4x	6.3x	4.7x	4.0x	Ba3	BB-
Crespin International	MCR	Dec-31	1.80	10%	6%	4%	0%	28%	2.1x	1.8x	5.7x	4.4x	3.9x	Ba3	BB-
Mean			1.57	12%	8%	4%	2%	33%	2.1x	1.7x	5.5x	4.2x	3.9x		
Median			1.55	12%	8%	4%	3%	34%	2.1x	1.8x	5.7x	4.4x	3.9x		
Overall															
Mean			1.51	16%	12%	5%	1%	37%	2.0x	1.4x	8.2x	6.3x	6.0x		
Median			1.50	15%	10%	5%	1%	37%	1.8x	1.4x	8.4x	7.0x	6.2x		
High			1.90	30%	29%	9%	4%	57%	3.0x	2.4x	13.8x	10.7x	9.9x		
Low			1.14	10%	6%	3%	0%	18%	1.1x	0.0x	4.2x	3.0x	2.9x		

Source: Company filings, Bloomberg, Consensus Estimates
Note: Last twelve months data based on September 30, 2012. Estimated annual financial data based on a calendar year.

Step IV: Benchmark the Comparable Companies

ValueCo Corporation
Comparable Companies Analysis
($ in millions, except per share data)

Company	Ticker	Current Share Price	% of 52-wk. High	Equity Value	Enterprise Value	EV / LTM Sales	2012E Sales	2013E Sales	LTM EBITDA	2012E EBITDA	2013E EBITDA	LTM EBIT	2012E EBIT	2013E EBIT	LTM EBITDA Margin	Total Debt / EBITDA	Price / LTM EPS	2012E EPS	2013E EPS	LT EPS Growth
Tier I: Specialty Chemicals																				
BuyerCo	BUY	$70.00	91%	$9,800	$11,600	1.8x	1.7x	1.6x	8.0x	7.8x	7.3x	9.1x	8.8x	8.2x	22%	1.5x	13.9x	13.5x	12.5x	7%
Sherman Co.	SHR	40.00	76%	5,600	8,101	1.4x	1.4x	1.3x	7.7x	7.7x	7.2x	10.8x	10.7x	10.1x	18%	3.0x	13.4x	12.8x	11.8x	9%
Pearl Corp.	PRL	68.50	95%	5,172	5,856	1.4x	1.4x	1.3x	7.0x	7.0x	6.5x	9.4x	9.4x	8.7x	20%	1.8x	15.9x	14.7x	13.4x	11%
Gasparro Corp.	JDG	50.00	80%	5,000	6,750	1.4x	1.4x	1.3x	7.5x	7.1x	6.6x	9.3x	8.8x	8.2x	19%	2.1x	12.9x	11.2x	10.0x	12%
Kumra Inc.	KUM	52.50	88%	4,852	5,345	1.7x	1.7x	1.5x	8.0x	7.9x	7.4x	10.6x	10.4x	9.7x	21%	1.3x	19.5x	16.6x	14.4x	10%
Mean						1.5x	1.5x	1.4x	7.7x	7.5x	7.0x	9.8x	9.6x	9.0x	20%	1.9x	15.1x	13.8x	12.4x	10%
Median						1.4x	1.4x	1.3x	7.7x	7.7x	7.2x	9.4x	9.4x	8.7x	20%	1.8x	13.9x	13.5x	12.5x	10%
Tier II: Commodity / Diversified Chemicals																				
Falloon Group	FLN	$31.00	87%	$7,480	$11,254	1.0x	1.0x	0.9x	6.9x	7.0x	6.7x	10.8x	11.0x	10.5x	14%	2.5x	16.1x	15.0x	13.1x	5%
Goodson Corp.	GDS	64.00	83%	4,160	5,660	1.2x	1.2x	1.1x	7.4x	7.5x	7.2x	10.8x	11.0x	10.4x	16%	2.9x	19.5x	18.6x	16.3x	9%
Pryor Industries	PRI	79.00	88%	3,926	4,166	1.1x	1.2x	1.1x	7.3x	7.4x	7.1x	9.9x	10.1x	9.6x	15%	1.1x	17.3x	16.9x	15.4x	10%
Lanzarone Global	LNZ	32.25	80%	3,230	3,823	1.0x	1.0x	1.0x	6.6x	6.7x	6.4x	8.9x	9.0x	8.6x	16%	1.3x	13.9x	12.9x	11.7x	8%
McMenamin & Co.	MCM	33.50	80%	3,193	3,193	1.0x	0.9x	0.8x	9.0x	8.4x	7.5x	14.2x	13.1x	11.8x	11%	1.2x	26.8x	23.3x	20.3x	12%
Mean						1.1x	1.1x	1.0x	7.4x	7.4x	7.0x	10.9x	10.8x	10.2x	14%	1.8x	18.7x	17.3x	15.3x	9%
Median						1.0x	1.0x	1.0x	7.3x	7.4x	7.1x	10.8x	11.0x	10.4x	15%	1.3x	17.3x	16.9x	15.4x	9%
Tier III: Small-Cap Chemicals																				
S. Momper & Co.	MOMP	$28.00	95%	$2,240	$2,921	1.4x	1.4x	1.2x	7.7x	7.4x	6.7x	9.9x	9.5x	8.6x	18%	2.6x	17.2x	17.5x	16.2x	5%
Adler Worldwide	ADL	10.50	80%	1,217	1,463	0.9x	1.0x	0.9x	6.0x	6.1x	5.8x	8.0x	8.1x	7.7x	16%	1.6x	13.7x	14.8x	13.7x	7%
Schachter & Sons	STM	4.50	89%	1,125	1,674	1.0x	0.9x	0.8x	7.0x	6.5x	5.7x	9.8x	9.1x	7.9x	14%	2.5x	14.8x	13.6x	12.2x	11%
Girshin Holdings	MGP	50.00	67%	1,035	1,298	0.8x	0.8x	0.7x	7.3x	6.8x	6.1x	11.5x	10.7x	9.7x	11%	1.8x	20.0x	18.9x	17.2x	8%
Crespin International	MCR	27.00	80%	872	1,222	0.8x	0.8x	0.7x	6.4x	6.0x	5.4x	9.2x	8.6x	7.7x	13%	2.1x	14.2x	14.0x	12.7x	6%
Mean						1.0x	1.0x	0.9x	6.9x	6.6x	5.9x	9.7x	9.2x	8.3x	14%	2.1x	16.0x	15.7x	14.4x	7%
Median						0.9x	0.9x	0.8x	7.0x	6.5x	5.8x	9.8x	9.1x	7.9x	14%	2.1x	14.8x	14.8x	13.7x	7%
Overall																				
Mean						1.1x	1.1x	1.0x	7.3x	7.2x	6.7x	10.3x	10.0x	9.3x	16%	1.9x	17.0x	16.0x	14.4x	9%
Median						1.0x	1.0x	1.0x	7.3x	7.4x	6.7x	9.9x	9.8x	9.2x	16%	1.8x	16.6x	15.8x	14.1x	9%
High						1.8x	1.7x	1.6x	9.0x	8.4x	7.5x	14.2x	13.1x	11.8x	22%	3.0x	26.8x	23.3x	20.3x	12%
Low						0.8x	0.8x	0.7x	6.0x	6.0x	5.4x	8.0x	8.1x	7.7x	11%	1.1x	12.9x	11.2x	10.0x	5%

Source: Company filings, Bloomberg, Consensus Estimates
Note: Last twelve months data based on September 30, 2012. Estimated annual financial data based on a calendar year.

Step IV: Benchmark the Comparable Companies

ValueCo Corporation
Comparable Companies Analysis
($ in millions, except per share data)

Company	Ticker	Current Share Price	% of 52-wk. High	Equity Value	Enterprise Value	EV / EBITDA 2012E	EV / EBITDA 2013E	2012E EBITDA Margin	LTM Debt / EBITDA	LTM Int Exp / EBITDA	P/E 2012E	P/E 2013E	LT EPS Growth	Div Yield	FCF Yield 2012E	FCF Yield 2013E
Tier I: Specialty Chemicals																
BuyerCo	BUY	$70.00	91%	$9,800	$11,600	7.8x	7.3x	22%	1.5x	10.1x	13.5x	12.5x	7%	0.0%	7.2%	7.8%
Sherman Co.	SHR	$40.00	76%	5,600	8,101	7.7x	7.2x	18%	3.0x	13.8x	12.8x	11.8x	9%	1.8%	8.8%	9.7%
Pearl Corp.	PRL	$68.50	95%	5,172	5,856	7.0x	6.5x	20%	1.8x	8.4x	14.7x	13.4x	11%	0.0%	8.1%	8.9%
Gasparro Corp.	JDG	$50.00	80%	5,000	6,750	7.1x	6.6x	19%	2.1x	9.0x	11.2x	10.0x	12%	2.0%	7.0%	7.5%
Kumra Inc.	KUM	$52.50	88%	4,852	5,345	7.9x	7.4x	21%	1.3x	11.0x	16.6x	14.4x	10%	1.5%	5.8%	6.4%
Mean						7.5x	7.0x	20%	1.9x	10.5x	13.8x	12.4x	10%	1.1%	7.4%	8.1%
Median						7.7x	7.2x	20%	1.8x	10.1x	13.5x	12.5x	10%	1.5%	7.2%	7.8%
Tier II: Commodity / Diversified Chemicals																
Falloon Group	FLN	$31.00	87%	$7,480	$11,254	7.0x	6.7x	14%	2.5x	5.7x	15.0x	13.1x	5%	2.6%	7.0%	7.7%
Goodson Corp.	GDS	$64.00	83%	4,160	5,660	7.5x	7.2x	16%	2.9x	4.2x	18.6x	16.3x	9%	1.0%	5.7%	6.3%
Pryor Industries	PRI	$79.00	88%	3,926	4,166	7.4x	7.1x	15%	1.1x	11.1x	16.9x	15.4x	10%	0.8%	6.9%	7.5%
Lanzarone Global	LNZ	$32.25	95%	3,230	3,823	6.7x	6.4x	16%	1.3x	10.7x	12.9x	11.7x	8%	0.0%	7.3%	8.0%
McMenamin & Co.	MCM	$33.50	80%	3,193	3,193	8.4x	7.5x	11%	1.2x	10.6x	23.3x	20.3x	12%	1.2%	5.4%	5.9%
Mean						7.4x	7.0x	14%	1.8x	8.5x	17.3x	15.3x	9%	1.1%	6.5%	7.1%
Median						7.4x	7.1x	15%	1.3x	10.6x	16.9x	15.4x	9%	1.0%	6.9%	7.5%
Tier III: Small-Cap Chemicals																
S. Momper & Co.	MOMP	$28.00	95%	$2,240	$2,921	7.4x	6.7x	18%	2.6x	4.5x	17.5x	16.2x	5%	3.7%	6.8%	7.4%
Adler Worldwide	ADL	$10.50	80%	1,217	1,463	6.1x	5.8x	16%	1.6x	6.2x	14.8x	13.7x	7%	4.0%	8.2%	8.9%
Schachter & Sons	STM	$4.50	89%	1,125	1,674	6.5x	5.7x	14%	2.5x	5.0x	13.6x	12.2x	11%	0.8%	5.2%	5.7%
Girshin Holdings	MGP	$50.00	67%	1,035	1,298	6.8x	6.1x	11%	1.8x	6.3x	18.9x	17.2x	8%	2.8%	7.1%	7.7%
Crespin International	MCR	$27.00	80%	872	1,222	6.0x	5.4x	13%	2.1x	5.7x	14.0x	12.7x	6%	0.0%	8.9%	9.7%
Mean						6.6x	5.9x	14%	2.1x	5.5x	15.7x	14.4x	7%	2.2%	7.2%	7.9%
Median						6.5x	5.8x	14%	2.1x	5.7x	14.8x	13.7x	7%	2.8%	7.1%	7.7%
Overall																
Mean						7.2x	6.6x	16%	2.0x	8.2x	15.6x	14.0x	9%	1.5%	7.0%	7.7%
Median						7.1x	6.7x	16%	1.8x	8.4x	14.8x	13.4x	9%	1.2%	7.0%	7.7%
High						8.4x	7.5x	22%	3.0x	13.8x	23.3x	20.3x	12%	4.0%	8.9%	9.7%
Low						6.0x	5.4x	11%	1.1x	4.2x	11.2x	10.0x	5%	0.0%	5.2%	5.7%

Source: Company filings, Bloomberg, Consensus Estimates

Step V: Determine Valuation

- Trading multiples for comparable companies serve as basis for deriving an appropriate valuation <u>range</u> for target
- Use means and medians of most relevant multiple for sector (e.g., EV/EBITDA or P/E) to extrapolate range of multiples
  - Focus on two-to-three closest comparables to frame ultimate valuation
- Must also determine which period financial data is most relevant for calculating trading multiples
  - Depends on sector, point in business cycle, and comfort with consensus estimates
  - LTM, one-year forward, or even two-year forward financials

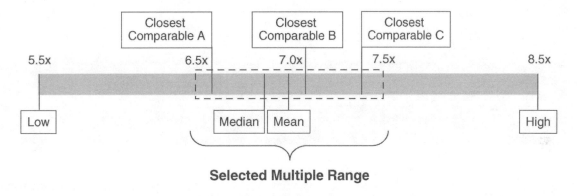

Step V: Determine Valuation

Valuation Implied by EV/EBITDA

- EV/EBITDA multiple range translates into implied range for enterprise value, equity value, and share price

($ in millions, except per share data)

EBITDA	Financial Metric	Multiple Range		Implied Enterprise Value		Less: Net Debt	Implied Equity Value		Fully Diluted Shares	Implied Share Price	
LTM	$200	7.0x	– 8.0x	$1,400	– $1,600	(500)	$900	– $1,100	100	$9.00	– $11.00
2012E	215	6.5x	– 7.5x	1,398	– 1,613	(500)	898	– 1,113	100	$8.98	– $11.13
2013E	230	6.0x	– 7.0x	1,380	– 1,610	(500)	880	– 1,110	100	$8.80	– $11.10

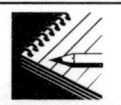

Step V: Determine Valuation

Valuation Implied by P/E

- P/E ratio translates into implied share price and enterprise value range
  - Implied Share Price
    - Begin with net income and build up to implied equity value
    - Equity value is then divided by fully diluted shares outstanding to calculate implied share price (public company's only)

($ in millions, except per share data)

Net Income	Financial Metric	Multiple Range			Implied Equity Value			Fully Diluted Shares	Implied Share Price		
LTM	$70	13.0x	–	16.0x	$910	–	$1,120	100	$9.10	–	$11.20
2012E	75	12.0x	–	15.0x	900	–	1,125	100	$9.00	–	$11.25
2013E	80	11.0x	–	14.0x	880	–	1,120	100	$8.80	–	$11.20

Step V: Determine Valuation

Valuation Implied by P/E (continued)

- Implied Enterprise Value
  - Add net debt to equity value

($ in millions)

Net Income	Financial Metric	Multiple Range		Implied Equity Value		Plus: Net Debt	Implied Enterprise Value	
LTM	$70	13.0x	– 16.0x	$910	– $1,120	500	$1,410	– $1,620
2012E	75	12.0x	– 15.0x	900	– 1,125	500	1,400	– 1,625
2013E	80	11.0x	– 14.0x	880	– 1,120	500	1,380	– 1,620

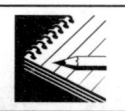

Step V: Determine Valuation

- Implied valuation range typically displayed in "football field" format
  - Eventual comparison against other valuation methodologies

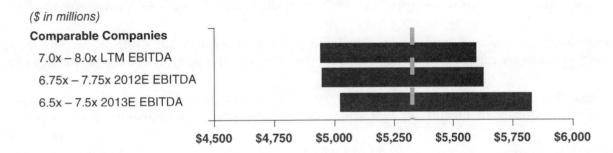

($ in millions)

Comparable Companies

7.0x – 8.0x LTM EBITDA

6.75x – 7.75x 2012E EBITDA

6.5x – 7.5x 2013E EBITDA

$4,500 $4,750 $5,000 $5,250 $5,500 $5,750 $6,000

Key Pros and Cons

Pros

- **Market-based** – information used to derive valuation for the target is based on actual public market data, thereby reflecting the market's growth and risk expectations, as well as overall sentiment
- **Relativity** – easily measurable and comparable versus other companies
- **Quick and convenient** – valuation can be determined on the basis of a few easy-to-calculate inputs
- **Current** – valuation is based on prevailing market data, which can be updated on a daily (or intraday) basis

Cons

- **Market-based** – valuation that is completely market-based can be skewed during periods of irrational exuberance or bearishness
- **Absence of relevant comparables** – "pure play" comparables may be difficult to identify or even non-existent, especially if the target operates in a niche sector, in which case the valuation implied by trading comps may be less meaningful
- **Potential disconnect from cash flow** – valuation based on prevailing market conditions or expectations may have significant disconnect from the valuation implied by a company's projected cash flow generation (e.g., DCF analysis)
- **Company-specific issues** – valuation of the target is based on the valuation of other companies, which may fail to capture target-specific strengths, weaknesses, opportunities, and risks

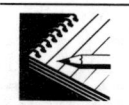

Chapter 2
Precedent Transactions Analysis

Precedent Transactions Analysis Steps

Step I.   Select the Universe of Comparable Acquisitions

Step II.   Locate the Necessary Deal-Related and Financial Information

Step III.   Spread Key Statistics, Ratios, and Transaction Multiples

Step IV.   Benchmark the Comparable Acquisitions

Step V.   Determine Valuation

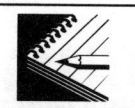

Overview of Precedent Transactions Analysis

- Employs multiples-based approach to derive an implied valuation range for target
- Premised on multiples paid for comparable companies in prior transactions
- Broad range of applications
  - Most notably to help determine potential sale price range for company in M&A or restructuring transaction
- Selection of appropriate universe of comparable acquisitions is foundation for performing precedent transactions
  - Best comparable acquisitions involve companies similar to target on fundamental level
  - Most recent transactions are most relevant as they likely took place under similar market conditions to contemplated transaction
- Under normal market conditions, transaction comps tend to provide a higher multiple range than trading comps for two principal reasons
  - Buyers pay "control premium" when purchasing another company
  - Strategic buyers often have opportunity to realize synergies
- Potential buyers and sellers look closely at multiples that have been paid for comparable acquisitions

Step I: Select the Universe of Comparable Acquisitions

Screen for Comparable Acquisitions

- Initial goal when screening for comparable acquisitions is to locate as many potential transactions as possible for a relevant, recent time period and then refine the universe

Sources for Creating an Initial List of Comparable Acquisitions

Search M&A databases

Review equity and fixed income research reports

Examine target's M&A history

Search merger proxies for comparable acquisitions

Revisit target's universe of comparable companies

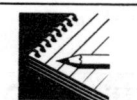

Step I: Select the Universe of Comparable Acquisitions

Examine Other Considerations

- Important to gain better understanding of specific circumstances and context for each transaction
  - Generally does not change list of comparable acquisitions to be examined
  - Helps interpret the multiple paid, as well as its relevance to the target being valued

Market Conditions

- Refers to business and economic environment, as well as prevailing state of capital markets, at time of given transaction
  - Conditions directly affect availability and cost of acquisition financing and influence price an acquirer is willing, or able, to pay
  - Affect buyer and seller confidence with respect to undertaking transaction

Step I: Select the Universe of Comparable Acquisitions

Examine Other Considerations (continued)

- Must be viewed within context of specific sectors and cycles (e.g., housing, steel, and technology)

| Height of technology bubble in late 1990s and early 2000s | Record low-rate debt financing environment of mid 2000s |

Deal Dynamics

1) Was the acquirer a *strategic buyer* or a *financial sponsor*?
   - Strategic buyers traditionally can pay higher purchase prices than financial sponsors due to potential ability to realize synergies

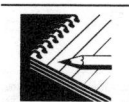

Examine Other Considerations (continued)

2) What were the buyer's and seller's *motivations* for the transaction?
   - Strategic buyer may pay higher price for asset if substantial synergies and/or asset is critical to strategic plan ("scarcity value")
   - Sponsor may be more aggressive on price if synergies can be realized by combining target with an existing portfolio company
   - Corporation in need of cash that is selling non-core business may prioritize speed of execution and certainty of completion

3) Was target sold through *auction process* or *negotiated sale*? Was the nature of the deal *friendly* or *hostile*?
   - Auctions are designed to maximize competitive dynamics with goal of producing best offer at highest possible price
   - Hostile situations may also produce higher purchase prices
   - Merger of equals transactions usually forego premium

4) What was the *purchase consideration* (i.e., mix of cash and stock)?
   - All-stock transaction tends to result in lower valuation than all-cash transaction as target shareholders retain equity interest in combined entity
   - Target shareholders require more upfront compensation in all-cash transaction as they are unable to participate in value creation opportunities that result from combining the two companies

Step II: Locate the Necessary Deal-Related and Financial Information

- Invariably easier for transactions involving public targets due to SEC disclosure requirements
  - Private companies with publicly registered debt securities
- Availability of information for M&A transactions involving private targets typically depends whether public securities were used as acquisition financing
  - Challenging and sometimes impossible to obtain complete (or any) financial information necessary to determine transaction multiples
- Public acquirers may safeguard information for competitive reasons and only disclose information that is required by law or regulation

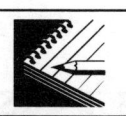

Public Targets

Sources for Public Target Information

- Proxy Statement for One-Step Merger Transaction – document that public company sends to shareholders prior to shareholder meeting containing material information regarding potential transaction that shareholders are expected to vote on
- Schedule TO/Schedule 14D-9 – Acquirer must file TO when they offer to buy shares directly from target's shareholders and target must file Schedule 14D-9 within ten business days with recommendation to shareholders
- Registration Statement/Prospectus (S-4, 424B) – required when public acquirer issues shares as part of purchase consideration for target in order for shares to be freely tradeable by target's shareholders
- Schedule 13E-3 – schedule that must be filed by publicly-traded company when they become "private"
- 8-K – acquisition is required to be reported in 8-K if assets, income, or value of target comprise 10% or greater of acquirer's
- 10-K and 10-Q – primary sources for locating information necessary to calculate relevant LTM financial statistics, including adjustments for non-recurring items and significant recent events
- Equity and Fixed Income Research – provide helpful deal insight, including information on pro forma adjustments and expected synergies

Step II: Locate the Necessary Deal-Related and Financial Information

Private Targets

Sources for Private Target Information

- Private target (i.e., a non-public filer) is not required to publicly file documentation in M&A transaction
  - Sourcing of relevant information on private targets depends on type of acquirer and/or acquisition financing
- When public acquirer buys private target it may be required to file certain disclosure documents
  - Registration Statement/Prospectus if using public securities as part of purchase consideration
  - Proxy Statement if issuing shares in excess of 20% of pre-deal shares
  - 8-K upon announcement and completion of material transaction
- Availability of information for LBOs of private targets depends whether public debt securities (e.g. high yield bonds) are issued
  - S-4 contains relevant data on purchase price and target financials to spread the precedent transaction
- Private acquirer/private target transactions (including LBOs) involving nonpublic financing
  - Most difficult transactions for which to obtain information because there are no SEC disclosure requirements
  - Rely on less formal sources for deal information, such as company website, press releases, news articles, and trade journals

Step III: Spread Key Statistics, Ratios, and Transaction Multiples

- As with trading comps, for precedent transactions an input sheet is created for each comparable acquisition, which, in turn, feeds into summary output sheets used for the benchmarking analysis.

Input Sheet	Output Sheets
<ul><li>Enter key transaction data relating to purchase price, form of consideration, and target financial statistics into input page</li><li>Feeds into summary output sheets used to benchmark the transaction multiples</li><li>Designed to assist in calculating the key financial statistics, ratios, and multiples for the precedent transactions universe</li></ul>	<ul><li>Summary of key financial data for the transaction multiples</li><li>Data is presented in clear and succinct format for easy comparison</li><li>Serves as basis for identifying, analyzing and comparing transaction multiples</li></ul>

Step III: Spread Key Statistics, Ratios, and Transaction Multiples

Calculation of Key Financial Statistics and Ratios

- Process for spreading the key financial statistics and ratios for precedent transactions is similar to that outlined in Chapter 1 for comparable companies
- Certain nuances for calculating equity value and enterprise value in precedent transactions including under different purchase consideration scenarios
- Analysis of premiums paid and synergies

Calculation of Key Financial Statistics and Ratios (continued)

- Equity Value ("equity purchase price" or "offer value")
  - Offer price per share is multiplied by the target's fully diluted shares outstanding
  - Calculated in a similar manner as that for comparable companies
    - Based on the announced offer price per share as opposed to the closing share price on a given day
    - All outstanding in-the-money options and warrants are converted at their weighted average strike prices regardless of whether they are exercisable or not
    - Out-of-the money options and warrants are not assumed to be converted

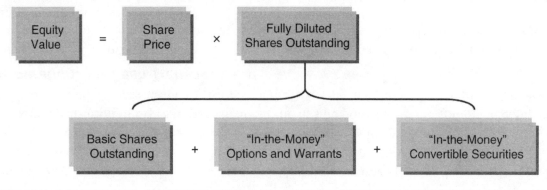

Step III: Spread Key Statistics, Ratios, and Transaction Multiples

Purchase Consideration

- Refers to the mix of cash, stock, and/or other securities that the acquirer offers to the target's shareholders
- Form of consideration can affect the target shareholders' perception of the value embedded in the offer
  - Some shareholders may prefer cash over stock as payment due to its guaranteed value, some shareholders may prefer stock compensation in order to participate in the upside potential of the combined companies
  - Tax consequences and other issues may also play a decisive role in guiding shareholder preferences

Purchase Consideration: All-Cash Transaction

- Acquirer makes an offer to purchase all or a portion of the target's shares outstanding for cash
- Makes for a simple equity value calculation by multiplying the cash offer price per share by the number of fully diluted shares outstanding
- Represents the cleanest form of currency and certainty of value for all shareholders
- Triggers a taxable event as opposed to the exchange or receipt of shares of stock

CLEVELAND, Ohio – June 15, 2012 – AcquirerCo and TargetCo today announced the two companies have entered into a definitive agreement for AcquirerCo to acquire the equity of TargetCo, a publicly held company, in an all-cash transaction at a price of approximately $1 billion, or $20.00 per share. The acquisition is subject to TargetCo shareholder and regulatory approvals and other customary closing conditions, and is expected to close in the fourth quarter of 2012.

Step III: Spread Key Statistics, Ratios, and Transaction Multiples

Purchase Consideration: Stock-for-Stock Transaction

- Fixed Exchange Ratio – defines the number of shares of the acquirer's stock to be exchanged for each share of the target's stock

> CLEVELAND, Ohio – June 15, 2012 – AcquirerCo has announced a definitive agreement to acquire TargetCo in an all-stock transaction valued at $1 billion. Under the terms of the agreement, which has been approved by both boards of directors, TargetCo stockholders will receive, at a fixed exchange ratio, 0.50 shares of AcquirerCo common stock for every share of TargetCo common stock. Based on AcquirerCo's stock price on June 14, 2012 of $40.00, this represents a price of $20.00 per share of TargetCo common stock.

- Offer price per share is calculated by multiplying the exchange ratio by the share price of the acquirer, typically one day prior to announcement

$$\text{Offer Price per Share} = \text{Exchange Ratio} \times \text{Acquirer's Share Price}$$

$$\text{Equity Value} = \text{Exchange Ratio} \times \text{Acquirer's Share Price} \times \text{Target's Fully Diluted Shares Outstanding}$$

Purchase Consideration: Stock-for-Stock Transaction (continued)

- Offer price per share (value to target) moves in line with the underlying share price of the acquirer
  - Amount of the acquirer's shares received is constant
  - Shares received by the target and the respective ownership percentages for the acquirer and target remain fixed
  - Fixed regardless of share price movement between execution of the definitive agreement ("signing") and transaction close

Fixed Exchange Ratio – Value to Target and Shares Received

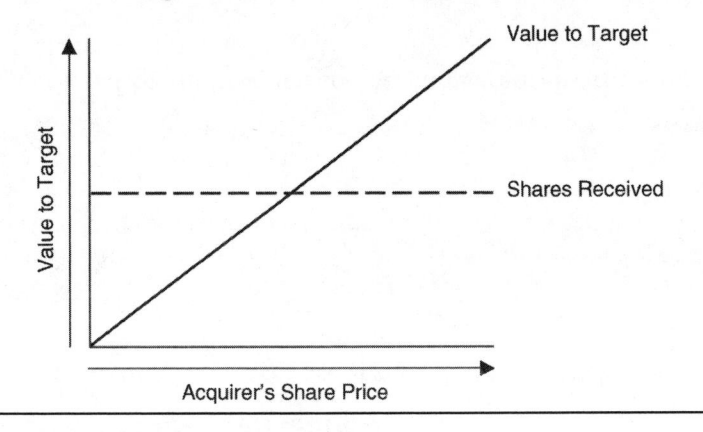

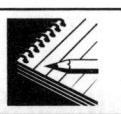

Purchase Consideration: Stock-for-Stock Transaction (continued)

- Floating Exchange Ratio – represents the set dollar amount per share that the acquirer has agreed to pay for each share of the target's stock in the form of shares of the acquirer's stock

> CLEVELAND, Ohio – June 15, 2012 – AcquirerCo and TargetCo today announced the execution of a definitive agreement pursuant to which AcquirerCo will acquire TargetCo in an all-stock transaction. Pursuant to the agreement, TargetCo stockholders will receive $20.00 of AcquirerCo common stock for each share of TargetCo common stock they hold. The number of AcquirerCo shares to be issued to TargetCo stockholders will be calculated based on the average closing price of AcquirerCo common stock for the 30 trading days immediately preceding the third trading day before the closing of the transaction.

- Dollar offer price per share (value to target) is set and the number of shares exchanged fluctuates in accordance with the movement of the acquirer's share price
- Number of shares to be exchanged based on average of acquirer's share price for specified time period prior to transaction close

Purchase Consideration: Stock-for-Stock Transaction (continued)

- Structure presents target shareholders with greater certainty in terms of value received
  - Acquirer assumes the full risk of a decline in its share price (assuming no structural protections for the acquirer)

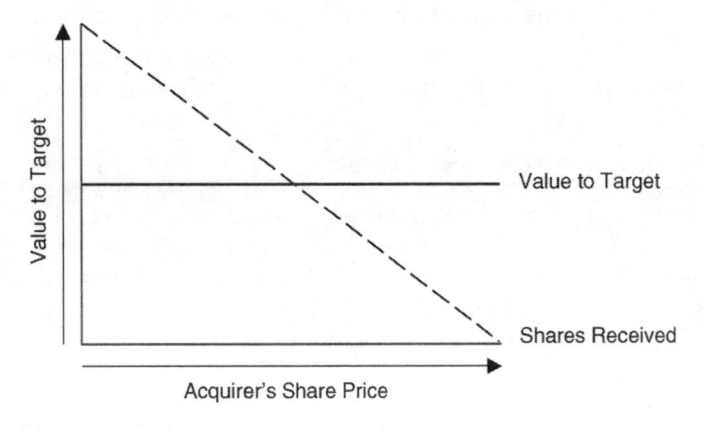

Floating Exchange Ratio – Value to Target and Shares Received

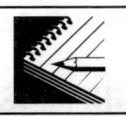

Step III: Spread Key Statistics, Ratios, and Transaction Multiples

Purchase Consideration: Cash and Stock Transaction

- Cash and Stock Transaction – acquirer offers a combination of cash and stock as purchase consideration

> CLEVELAND, Ohio –June 15, 2012 –AcquirerCo and TargetCo announced today that they signed a definitive agreement whereby AcquirerCo will acquire TargetCo for a purchase price of approximately $1 billion in a mix of cash and AcquirerCo stock. Under the terms of the agreement, which was unanimously approved by the boards of directors of both companies, TargetCo stockholders will receive $10.00 in cash and 0.25 shares of AcquirerCo common stock for each outstanding TargetCo share. Based on AcquirerCo's closing price of $40.00 on June 14, 2012, AcquirerCo will issue an aggregate of approximately 12.5 million shares of its common stock and pay an aggregate of approximately $500 million in cash in the transaction.

- – Cash portion of the offer represents a fixed value per share for target shareholders
- – Stock portion of the offer can be set according to either a fixed or floating exchange ratio

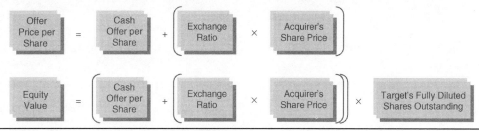

Step III: Spread Key Statistics, Ratios, and Transaction Multiples

Calculation of Key Financial Statistics and Ratios

- Enterprise Value ("transaction value")
  - Total value offered by the acquirer for the target's equity interests plus assumption or refinancing of the target's net debt
  - Calculated for precedent transactions in the same manner as for comparable companies – sum of equity, net debt, preferred stock, and noncontrolling interest

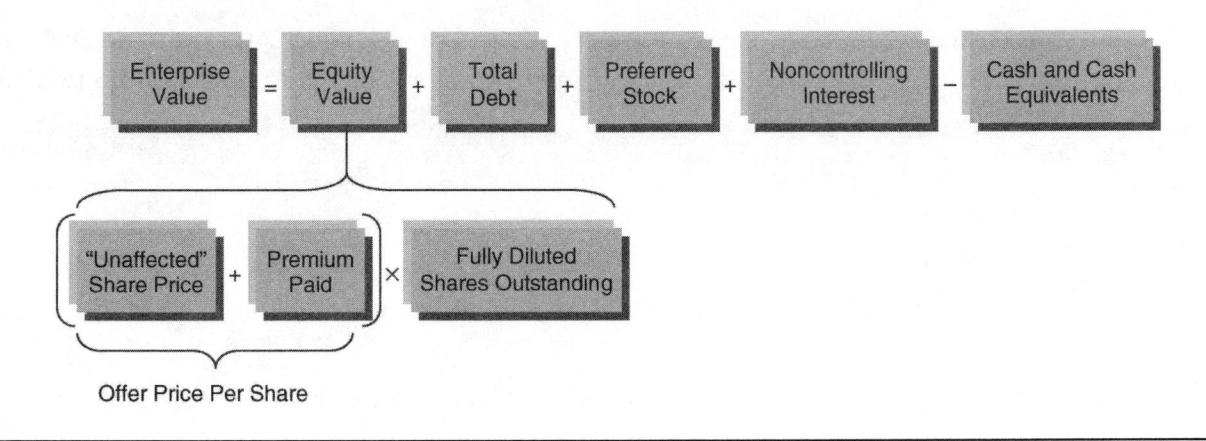

Step III: Spread Key Statistics, Ratios, and Transaction Multiples

Calculation of Key Transaction Multiples

- Key transaction multiples used in transaction comps mirror those used for trading comps
- Equity value used as multiple of net income (or offer price per share as a multiple of diluted EPS)
- Enterprise value (or transaction value) is used as multiple of EBITDA, EBIT, and to a lesser extent sales
- Multiples in precedent transactions are typically higher than those in trading comps
  - Premium paid for control
  - Synergies
- Multiples for precedent transactions typically calculated on basis of actual LTM financial statistics available at the time of announcement
  - Full projections that an acquirer uses to frame its purchase price decision are generally not public and subject to a confidentiality agreement
  - Buyers are often hesitant to give sellers full credit for projected financial performance as they assume the risk for realization.
- Source the information necessary to calculate the target's LTM financials directly from SEC filings
  - Data needs to be adjusted for non-recurring items and recent events in order to calculate clean multiples that reflect the target's normalized performance

Step III: Spread Key Statistics, Ratios, and Transaction Multiples

Equity Value Multiples

- Offer Price per Share-to-LTM EPS / Equity Value-to-LTM Net Income
  - Most broadly used equity value multiple is the P/E ratio
  - Offer price per share divided by LTM diluted earnings per share (or equity value divided by LTM net income)

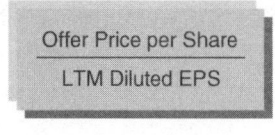
$$\frac{\text{Offer Price per Share}}{\text{LTM Diluted EPS}}$$

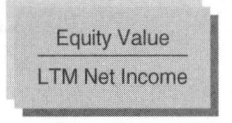
$$\frac{\text{Equity Value}}{\text{LTM Net Income}}$$

Enterprise Value Multiples

- Enterprise Value-to-LTM EBITDA, EBIT, and Sales
  - Enterprise value is used in the numerator when calculating multiples for financial statistics that apply to both debt and equity holders
  - EV/LTM EBITDA being the most prevalent
  - Certain sectors may rely on additional or other metrics to drive valuation

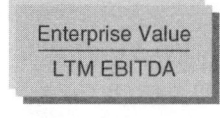
$$\frac{\text{Enterprise Value}}{\text{LTM EBITDA}}$$

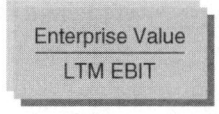
$$\frac{\text{Enterprise Value}}{\text{LTM EBIT}}$$

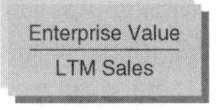
$$\frac{\text{Enterprise Value}}{\text{LTM Sales}}$$

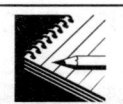

Premium Paid

- Incremental dollar amount per share that the acquirer offers relative to the target's unaffected share price
- Important to use the target's unaffected share price so as to isolate the true effect of the purchase offer
  - Closing share price on day prior to the official transaction announcement typically serves as good proxy for the unaffected share price
  - Examine offer price per share relative to target's share price at multiple time intervals prior to transaction announcement (e.g., one trading day, seven calendar days, and 30 calendar days or more)
  - Isolate the effects of market gyrations and potential share price "creep" due to rumors or information leakage regarding the deal

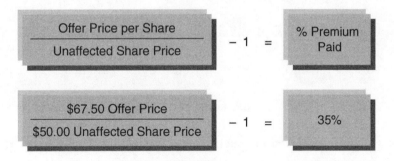

Step III: Spread Key Statistics, Ratios, and Transaction Multiples

Synergies

- Expected cost savings, growth opportunities, and other financial benefits that occur as a result of the combination of two businesses
- Assessment of synergies is most relevant for transactions where strategic buyer is purchasing target in related business
- Represent tangible value to the acquirer in the form of future cash flow and earnings above and beyond what can be achieved by the target on a standalone basis
  - Size and degree of likelihood for realizing potential synergies play an important role for the acquirer in framing the purchase price for a particular target
  - Amount of announced synergies provides important perspective on the purchase price and multiple paid
- Public acquirers often provide guidance on the nature and amount of expected synergies upon announcement of a material acquisition
- Helpful to note the announced expected synergies for each transaction where such information is available
  - Transaction multiples typically shown on basis of the target's reported LTM financial information (i.e., without adjusting for synergies)

Synergies (continued)

- May calculate adjusted multiples that reflect expected synergies
  - Typically involves adding the full effect of expected annual run-rate cost savings synergies (excluding costs to achieve) to an earnings metric in the denominator (e.g., EBITDA)

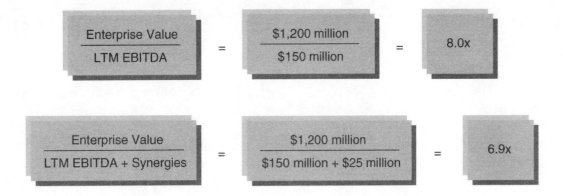

$$\frac{\text{Enterprise Value}}{\text{LTM EBITDA}} = \frac{\$1{,}200 \text{ million}}{\$150 \text{ million}} = 8.0x$$

$$\frac{\text{Enterprise Value}}{\text{LTM EBITDA} + \text{Synergies}} = \frac{\$1{,}200 \text{ million}}{\$150 \text{ million} + \$25 \text{ million}} = 6.9x$$

Step IV: Benchmark the Comparable Acquisitions

- In-depth study of the selected comparable acquisitions so as to determine those most relevant for valuing the target
- Re-examine the business profile and benchmark the key financial statistics and ratios for each of the acquired companies, with an eye toward identifying those most comparable to the target
- Each comparable acquisition is closely examined as part of the final refining of the universe, with the best comparable transactions identified and obvious outliers eliminated
- Recently consummated deal involving a direct competitor with a similar financial profile is typically more relevant than an older transaction from a different point in the business or credit cycle, or for a marginal player in the sector
- Thoughtful analysis weighs other considerations such as market conditions and deal dynamics in conjunction with the target's business and financial profile

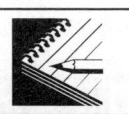

Step IV: Benchmark the Comparable Acquisitions

ValueCo Corporation
Precedent Transactions Analysis
(\$ in millions)

Date Announced	Acquirer	Target	Transaction Type	Purchase Consideration	Equity Value	Enterprise Value	Enterprise Value / LTM Sales	LTM EBITDA	LTM EBIT	LTM EBITDA Margin	Equity Value / LTM Net Income	Premiums Paid Days Prior to Unaffected 1	7	30
11/2/12	Pearl Corp.	Rosenbaum Industries	Public / Public	Cash	\$2,500	\$3,825	1.6x	8.5x	11.2x	19%	16.6x	35%	33%	37%
7/20/12	Goodson Corp.	Schneider & Co.	Public / Public	Cash / Stock	5,049	6,174	1.4x	8.1x	10.3x	18%	15.3x	29%	32%	31%
6/21/12	Domanski Capital	Ackerman Industries	Sponsor / Public	Cash	8,845	9,995	1.7x	8.0x	10.2x	21%	15.9x	35%	37%	39%
4/15/12	The Hochberg Group	Whalen Inc.	Sponsor / Private	Cash	1,250	1,350	1.9x	7.5x	9.6x	26%	15.2x	NA	NA	NA
8/8/11	Cole Manufacturing	Gordon Inc.	Public / Public	Stock	2,620	3,045	1.5x	9.0x	12.2x	17%	20.4x	47%	44%	49%
7/6/11	Eu-Han Capital	Rughwani International	Sponsor / Public	Cash	3,390	4,340	1.6x	7.8x	9.4x	21%	13.2x	38%	40%	43%
3/20/11	Lanzarone Global	Falk & Sons	Public / Private	Cash	8,750	10,350	1.7x	8.4x	10.5x	21%	16.0x	NA	NA	NA
11/9/10	Meisner Global Management	Kamras Brands	Sponsor / Private	Cash	1,765	2,115	1.5x	7.9x	9.3x	19%	13.8x	NA	NA	NA
6/22/10	Pryor, Inc.	ParkCo	Public / Private	Cash	6,450	8,700	1.1x	7.0x	7.9x	16%	11.8x	NA	NA	NA
4/15/10	Leicht & Co.	Bress Products	Public / Public	Stock	12,431	12,681	1.5x	8.2x	12.1x	19%	19.7x	29%	36%	34%
Mean							1.6x	8.0x	10.3x	19%	15.8x	36%	37%	39%
Median							1.6x	8.0x	10.3x	19%	15.6x	35%	36%	38%
High							1.9x	9.0x	12.2x	26%	20.4x	47%	44%	49%
Low							1.1x	7.0x	7.9x	16%	11.8x	29%	32%	31%

Source: Company filings

Step V: Determine Valuation

- Multiples of the selected comparable acquisitions universe are used to derive an implied valuation range for the target
- Key multiples driving valuation in precedent transactions tend to be enterprise value-to-LTM EBITDA and equity value-to-net income (or offer price per share-to-LTM diluted EPS, if public)
- Necessary to analyze the output and test conclusions

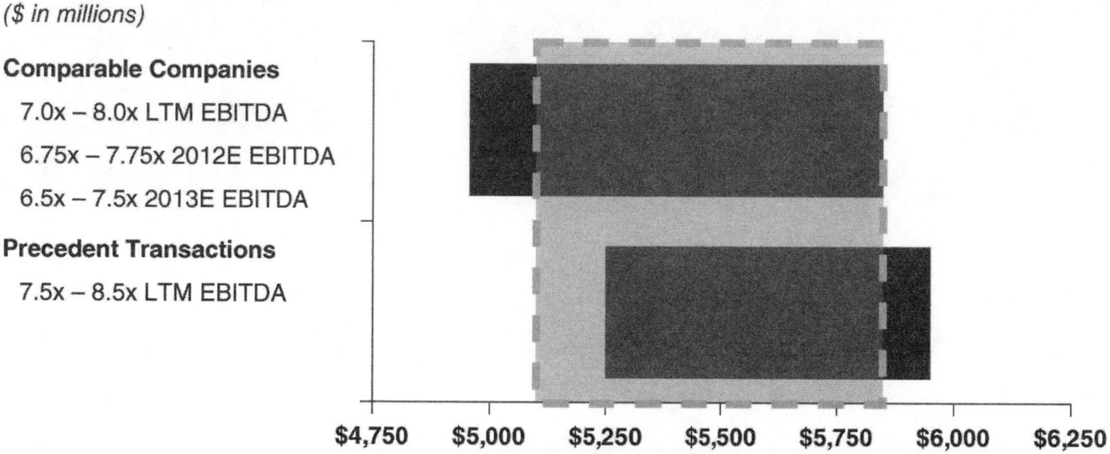

($ in millions)

Comparable Companies

  7.0x – 8.0x LTM EBITDA

  6.75x – 7.75x 2012E EBITDA

  6.5x – 7.5x 2013E EBITDA

Precedent Transactions

  7.5x – 8.5x LTM EBITDA

| $4,750 | $5,000 | $5,250 | $5,500 | $5,750 | $6,000 | $6,250 |

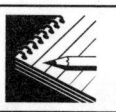

Key Pros and Cons

Pros

- **Market-based** – analysis is based on actual acquisition multiples and premiums paid for similar companies
- **Current** – recent transactions tend to reflect prevailing M&A, capital markets, and general economic conditions
- **Relativity** – multiples approach provides straightforward reference points across sectors and time periods
- **Simplicity** – key multiples for a few selected transactions can anchor valuation
- **Objectivity** – precedent-based and, therefore, avoids making assumptions about company's future performance

Cons

- **Market-based** – multiples may be skewed depending on capital markets and/or economic environment at the time of the transaction
- **Time lag** – precedent transactions, by definition, have occurred in the past and, therefore, may not be truly reflective of prevailing market conditions (e.g., the LBO boom in the mid-2000s vs. the ensuing credit crunch)
- **Existence of comparable acquisitions** – in some cases it may be difficult to find a robust universe of precedent transactions
- **Availability of information** – information may be insufficient to determine transaction multiples for many comparable acquisitions
- **Acquirer's basis for valuation** – multiple paid by the buyer may be based on expectations governing the target's future financial performance (which is typically not publicly disclosed) rather than on reported LTM financial information

Chapter 3
Discounted Cash Flow Analysis

Discounted Cash Flow Analysis Steps

Step I.   Study the Target and Determine Key Performance Drivers

Step II.   Project Free Cash Flow

Step III. Calculate Weighted Average Cost of Capital

Step IV.   Determine Terminal Value

Step V.   Calculate Present Value and Determine Valuation

Overview of Discounted Cash Flow Analysis

- Premised on the principle that the value of a company, division, business, or collection of assets ("target") can be derived from the present value of its projected free cash flow (FCF)
  - Projected FCF is derived from a variety of assumptions and judgments about a company's expected financial performance
  - Sales growth rates, profit margins, capital expenditures, and net working capital (NWC) requirements
- Valuation implied for a target by a DCF is also known as its "intrinsic value"
  - Serves as an important alternative to market-based valuation techniques
  - Valuable when there are limited (or no) pure play peer companies or comparable acquisitions
- Free Cash Flow
  - Typically projected for a period of five years; may be longer depending on company's sector, stage of development, and underlying predictability of its financial performance
  - Terminal value is used to capture the remaining value of the target beyond the projection period
  - Projected FCF and terminal value are discounted to the present at the target's weighted average cost of capital (WACC)
    - Discount rate commensurate with business and financial risks
    - Present value of the projected FCF and terminal value are summed to determine an enterprise value

Overview of Discounted Cash Flow Analysis

- WACC and terminal value assumptions typically have a substantial impact on the output
  - DCF output is viewed in terms of a valuation range based on a range of key input assumptions, rather than as a single value
  - The impact of these assumptions on valuation is tested using *sensitivity analysis*

Step I: Study the Target and Determine Key Performance Drivers

Study the Target

- Study and learn as much as possible about the target and its sector
  - Understanding of the target's business model, financial profile, value proposition for customers, end markets, competitors, and key risks is essential for developing a framework for valuation
  - Need to be able to craft (or support) a realistic set of financial projections, as well as WACC and terminal value assumptions
- SEC filings, investor presentations, and earnings call transcripts, and provide solid introduction to business and financial characteristics for public companies
  - Management's discussion and analysis (MD&A) is an important source of information as it provides a synopsis of the company's financial and operational performance during the prior reporting periods as well as management's outlook for the company
  - Equity research reports add additional color
- For private, non-filing companies or smaller divisions of public companies, need to rely on company management for materials containing basic business and financial information
  - Information is typically provided in the form of a confidential information memorandum (CIM) in organized M&A sale process
  - Alternative sources include company websites, trade journals and news articles, as well as SEC filings and research reports for public competitors, customers, and suppliers

---

Step I: Study the Target and Determine Key Performance Drivers

Determine Key Performance Drivers

- Determine key drivers of a company's performance
  - Particularly sales growth, profitability, and FCF generation
- Internal and external drivers
  - Internal – opening new facilities/stores, developing new products, securing new customer contracts, and improving operational and/or working capital efficiency
  - External – acquisitions, end market trends, consumer buying patterns, macroeconomic factors, or even legislative/regulatory changes
- Company's growth profile can vary significantly from that of its peers within the sector
  - Certain business models and management teams are more focused on expansion
- Profitability may also vary for companies within a given sector
  - Multitude of factors including management, brand, customer base, operational focus, product mix, sales/marketing strategy, scale, and technology
- FCF generation
  - Differences among peers in terms of capex (e.g., expansion projects or owned vs. leased machinery) and working capital efficiency

Step II: Project Free Cash Flow

- Unlevered FCF is the cash generated by a company after paying
  - Cash operating expenses
  - Associated taxes
  - Funding of capex and working capital
  - Prior to payment of any interest expense
- Independent of capital structure as it represents the cash available to all capital providers (both debt and equity holders)

Free Cash Flow Calculation

> Earnings Before Interest and Taxes
> Less: Taxes (at the Marginal Tax Rate)
>
> **Earnings Before Interest After Taxes**
> Plus: Depreciation & Amortization
> Less: Capital Expenditures
> Less: Increase/(Decrease) in Net Working Capital
>
> **Free Cash Flow**

Step II: Project Free Cash Flow

Considerations for Projecting Free Cash Flow

- Historical Performance
  - Provides valuable insight for developing defensible assumptions to project FCF
  - Past growth rates, profit margins, and other ratios are usually a reliable indicator of future performance, especially for mature companies in non-cyclical sectors
- Projection Period Length
  - Project the target's FCF for a period of five years depending on its sector, stage of development, and the predictability of its financial performance
  - Critical to project FCF to a point in the future where the target's financial performance reaches a steady state or normalized level
- Alternative Cases
  - Typically receive five years of financial projections directly from the company, which is usually labeled "Management Case"
  - Often make adjustments to management's projections that incorporate assumptions deemed more probable, known as the "Base Case," while also crafting upside and downside cases

---

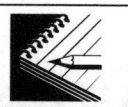

Step II: Project Free Cash Flow

Considerations for Projecting Free Cash Flow (continued)

- Projecting Financial Performance without Management Guidance
  - Often a DCF is performed without the benefit of receiving an initial set of projections
  - For publicly traded companies, consensus research estimates for financial statistics such as sales, EBITDA, and EBIT (which are generally provided for a future two- or three-year period) are typically used to form the basis for developing a set of projections
  - For private companies, a robust DCF often depends on receiving financial projections from company management

Step II: Project Free Cash Flow

Projection of Sales, EBITDA, and EBIT

- Sales Projections
    - Source top line projections for the first two or three years of the projection period from consensus estimates
    - Must derive growth rates in the outer years from alternative sources
        - Equity research may not provide financial projections beyond a future two- or three-year period
        - Industry reports and consulting studies provide estimates on longer-term sector trends and growth rates
    - Sales levels need to track movements of underlying commodity cycle for a highly cyclical business such as a steel or chemical company
        - Regardless of where in the cycle the projection period begins, crucial that the terminal year financial performance represents a normalized level

($ in millions, fiscal year ending December 31)

	Historical Period			CAGR	2012	Projection Period					CAGR
	2009	2010	2011	('09 - '11)		2013	2014	2015	2016	2017	('12 - '17)
Sales	$2,600.0	$2,900.0	$3,200.0	10.9%	$3,450.0	$3,708.8	$3,931.3	$4,127.8	$4,293.0	$4,421.7	5.1%
% growth	NA	11.5%	10.3%		7.8%	7.5%	6.0%	5.0%	4.0%	3.0%	

Step II: Project Free Cash Flow

Projection of Sales, EBITDA, and EBIT (continued)

- COGS and SG&A Projections
  - Rely upon historical COGS (gross margin) and SG&A levels (as a percentage of sales) and/or sources estimates from research to drive the initial years of the projection period
  - For the outer years of the projection period, common to hold gross margin and SG&A as a percentage of sales constant
  - For private companies, usually rely upon historical trends to drive gross profit and SG&A projections, typically holding margins constant at the prior historical year levels
  - In some cases, the DCF may be constructed on the basis of EBITDA and EBIT projections alone, thereby excluding line item detail for COGS and SG&A

($ in millions, fiscal year ending December 31)

| | Historical Period | | | CAGR | | Projection Period | | | | | CAGR |
	2009	2010	2011	('09 - '11)	2012	2013	2014	2015	2016	2017	('12 - '17)
Sales	$2,600.0	$2,900.0	$3,200.0	10.9%	$3,450.0	$3,708.8	$3,931.3	$4,127.8	$4,293.0	$4,421.7	5.1%
% growth	NA	11.5%	10.3%		7.8%	7.5%	6.0%	5.0%	4.0%	3.0%	
COGS	1,612.0	1,769.0	1,920.0		2,070.0	2,225.3	2,358.8	2,476.7	2,575.8	2,653.0	
% sales	62.0%	61.0%	60.0%		60.0%	60.0%	60.0%	60.0%	60.0%	60.0%	
Gross Profit	$988.0	$1,131.0	$1,280.0	13.8%	$1,380.0	$1,483.5	$1,572.5	$1,651.1	$1,717.2	$1,768.7	5.1%
% margin	38.0%	39.0%	40.0%		40.0%	40.0%	40.0%	40.0%	40.0%	40.0%	
SG&A	496.6	551.0	608.0		655.0	704.1	746.4	783.7	815.0	839.5	
% sales	19.1%	19.0%	19.0%		19.0%	19.0%	19.0%	19.0%	19.0%	19.0%	

Step II: Project Free Cash Flow

Projection of Sales, EBITDA, and EBIT (continued)

- EBITDA and EBIT Projections
  - EBITDA and EBIT projections for the future two- or three-year period are typically sourced from (or benchmarked against) consensus estimates for public companies
  - Common approach for projecting EBITDA and EBIT for the outer years is to hold their margins constant at the level represented by the last year provided by consensus estimates
  - Review historical trends as well as consensus estimates for peer companies for insight on projected margins for private companies

($ in millions, fiscal year ending December 31)

	Historical Period			CAGR		Projection Period					CAGR
	2009	2010	2011	('09 - '11)	2012	2013	2014	2015	2016	2017	('12 - '17)
Sales	$2,600.0	$2,900.0	$3,200.0	10.9%	$3,450.0	$3,708.8	$3,931.3	$4,127.8	$4,293.0	$4,421.7	5.1%
% growth	NA	11.5%	10.3%		7.8%	7.5%	6.0%	5.0%	4.0%	3.0%	
COGS	1,612.0	1,769.0	1,920.0		2,070.0	2,225.3	2,358.8	2,476.7	2,575.8	2,653.0	
% sales	62.0%	61.0%	60.0%		60.0%	60.0%	60.0%	60.0%	60.0%	60.0%	
Gross Profit	$988.0	$1,131.0	$1,280.0	13.8%	$1,380.0	$1,483.5	$1,572.5	$1,651.1	$1,717.2	$1,768.7	5.1%
% margin	38.0%	39.0%	40.0%		40.0%	40.0%	40.0%	40.0%	40.0%	40.0%	
SG&A	496.6	551.0	608.0		655.0	704.1	746.4	783.7	815.0	839.5	
% sales	19.1%	19.0%	19.0%		19.0%	19.0%	19.0%	19.0%	19.0%	19.0%	
EBITDA	$491.4	$580.0	$672.0	16.9%	$725.0	$779.4	$826.1	$867.4	$902.1	$929.2	5.1%
% margin	18.9%	20.0%	21.0%		21.0%	21.0%	21.0%	21.0%	21.0%	21.0%	
D&A	155.0	165.0	193.0		207.0	222.5	235.9	247.7	257.6	265.3	
% of sales	6.0%	5.7%	6.0%		6.0%	6.0%	6.0%	6.0%	6.0%	6.0%	
EBIT	$336.4	$415.0	$479.0	19.3%	$518.0	$556.9	$590.3	$619.8	$644.6	$663.9	5.1%
% margin	12.9%	14.3%	15.0%		15.0%	15.0%	15.0%	15.0%	15.0%	15.0%	

Step II: Project Free Cash Flow

Projection of Free Cash Flow

- EBIT typically serves as the springboard for calculating FCF
- To bridge from EBIT to FCF, several additional items need to be determined, including the marginal tax rate, D&A, capex, and changes in net working capital

EBIT to FCF

EBIT
Less: Taxes (at the Marginal Tax Rate)
EBIAT
Plus: Depreciation & Amortization
Less: Capital Expenditures
Less: Increase/(Decrease) in NWC
FCF

Step II: Project Free Cash Flow

Projection of Free Cash Flow (continued)

- Tax Projections
  - First step in calculating FCF from EBIT is to net out estimated taxes
  - Result is tax-effected EBIT, also known as EBIAT or NOPAT
  - Calculation involves multiplying EBIT by $(1 - t)$, where "t" is the target's marginal tax rate
  - Marginal tax rate of 35% to 40% is generally assumed for modeling purposes, but the company's actual tax rate (effective tax rate) in previous years can also serve as a reference point

($ in millions, fiscal year ending December 31)

	Historical Period			CAGR		Projection Period					CAGR
	2009	2010	2011	('09 - '11)	2012	2013	2014	2015	2016	2017	('12 - '17)
EBIT	$336.4	$415.0	$479.0	19.3%	$518.0	$556.9	$590.3	$619.8	$644.6	$663.9	5.1%
% margin	12.9%	14.3%	15.0%		15.0%	15.0%	15.0%	15.0%	15.0%	15.0%	
Taxes @ 38%						211.6	224.3	235.5	244.9	252.3	
EBIAT						$345.2	$366.0	$384.3	$399.6	$411.6	5.1%

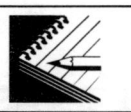

Step II: Project Free Cash Flow

Projection of Free Cash Flow (continued)

- Depreciation & Amortization Projections
  - Depreciation is a non-cash expense that approximates the reduction of the book value of a company's long-term fixed assets or property, plant, and equipment (PP&E) over an estimated useful life and reduces reported earnings
  - Amortization, like depreciation, is a non-cash expense that reduces the value of a company's definite life intangible assets and also reduces reported earnings
  - Some companies report D&A together as a separate line item on their income statement, but these expenses are more commonly included in COGS (especially for manufacturers of goods) and, to a lesser extent, SG&A
    - D&A is explicitly disclosed in the cash flow statement as well as the notes to a company's financial statements
  - D&A is a non-cash expense
    - Added back to EBIAT in the calculation of FCF
    - Decreases a company's reported earnings, but does not decrease its FCF

Step II: Project Free Cash Flow

Projection of Free Cash Flow (continued)

- Capital Expenditures Projections
  - Funds that a company uses to purchase, improve, expand, or replace physical assets such as buildings, equipment, facilities, machinery, and other assets
  - Capex is an expenditure as opposed to an expense
    - Capitalized on the balance sheet once the expenditure is made and then expensed over its useful life as depreciation through the company's income statement
    - As opposed to depreciation, capex represent actual cash outflows and, consequently, must be subtracted from EBIAT in the calculation of FCF (in the year in which the purchase is made)
  - Historical capex is disclosed directly on a company's cash flow statement under the investing activities section

($ in millions, fiscal year ending December 31)

	Historical Period			CAGR		Projection Period					CAGR
	2009	2010	2011	('09 - '11)	2012	2013	2014	2015	2016	2017	('12 - '17)
Sales	$2,600.0	$2,900.0	$3,200.0	10.9%	$3,450.0	$3,708.8	$3,931.3	$4,127.8	$4,293.0	$4,421.7	5.1%
% growth	NA	11.5%	10.3%		7.8%	7.5%	6.0%	5.0%	4.0%	3.0%	
Capex	114.4	116.0	144.0		155.3	166.9	176.9	185.8	193.2	199.0	
% sales	4.4%	4.0%	4.5%		4.5%	4.5%	4.5%	4.5%	4.5%	4.5%	

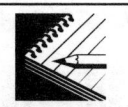

Step II: Project Free Cash Flow

Projection of Free Cash Flow (continued)

- Change in Net Working Capital Projections
  - Net working capital is defined as non-cash current assets less non-interest bearing current liabilities
  - Serves as a measure of how much cash a company needs to fund its operations on an ongoing basis
  - All of the necessary components to determine a company's NWC can be found on its balance sheet

Current Assets and Current Liabilities Components

Current Assets	Current Liabilities
▪ Accounts Receivable (A/R)	▪ Accounts Payable (A/P)
▪ Inventory	▪ Accrued Liabilities
▪ Prepaid Expenses and Other Current Assets	▪ Other Current Liabilities

Step II: Project Free Cash Flow

Projection of Free Cash Flow (continued)

- Change in NWC from year to year is important for calculating FCF as it represents an annual source or use of cash for the company

Calculation of Net Working Capital

$$NWC = \text{(Accounts Receivable + Inventory + Prepaid Expenses and Other Current Assets)} \\ \textit{less} \\ \text{(Accounts Payable + Accrued Liabilities + Other Current Liabilities)}$$

Calculation of a YoY Change in NWC

$$\Delta NWC = NWC_n - NWC_{(n-1)}$$

where: n = the most recent year
            $(n - 1)$ = the prior year

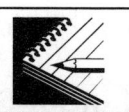

Step II: Project Free Cash Flow

Projection of Free Cash Flow (continued)

Current Assets: Accounts Receivable

- Refers to amounts owed to a company for its products and services sold on credit
- Customarily projected on the basis of days sales outstanding (DSO)

$$DSO = \frac{A/R}{Sales} \times 365$$

- DSO provides a gauge of how well a company is managing the collection of its A/R by measuring the number of days it takes to collect payment after the sale of a product or service
- DSO of 30 implies that the company, on average, receives payment 30 days after an initial sale is made
- The lower a company's DSO, the faster it receives cash from credit sales

Step II: Project Free Cash Flow

Projection of Free Cash Flow (continued)

Current Assets: Inventory

- Refers to the value of a company's raw materials, work in progress, and finished goods
- Customarily projected on the basis of days inventory held (DIH)

$$DIH = \frac{Inventory}{COGS} \times 365$$

- DIH measures the number of days it takes a company to sell its inventory
- DIH of 90 implies that, on average, it takes 90 days for the company to turn its inventory
- Companies strive to minimize DIH and turn their inventory as quickly as possible so as to minimize the amount of cash it ties up
- Inventory turns ratio measures the number of times a company turns over its inventory in a given year

$$Inventory\ Turns = COGS\ /\ Inventory$$

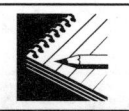

Step II: Project Free Cash Flow

Projection of Free Cash Flow (continued)

Current Assets: Prepaid Expenses and Other Current Assets

- Payments made by a company before a product has been delivered or a service has been performed
- Prepaid expenses and other current assets are typically projected as a percentage of sales in line with historical levels
- As with A/R and inventory, an increase in prepaid expenses and other current assets represents a use of cash

Current Liabilities: Accounts Payable

- Refers to amounts owed by a company for products and services already purchased
- Customarily projected on the basis of days payable outstanding (DPO)

$$DPO = \frac{A/P}{COGS} \times 365$$

- DPO measures the number of days it takes for a company to make payment on its outstanding purchases of goods and services

---

Step II: Project Free Cash Flow

Projection of Free Cash Flow (continued)

Current Liabilities: Accounts Payable (continued)

- DPO of 30 implies that the company takes 30 days on average to pay its suppliers
- The higher a company's DPO, the more time it has available to use its cash on hand for various business purposes before paying outstanding bills

Current Liabilities: Accrued Liabilities and Other Current Liabilities

- Expenses such as salaries, rent, interest, and taxes that have been incurred by a company but not yet paid
- As with prepaid expenses and other current assets, accrued liabilities and other current liabilities are typically projected as a percentage of sales in line with historical levels
- As with A/P, an increase in accrued liabilities and other current liabilities represents a source of cash

Step III: Calculate Weighted Average Cost of Capital

- WACC is a broadly accepted standard for use as the discount rate to calculate the present value of a company's projected FCF and terminal value
- WACC can also be thought of as an opportunity cost of capital or what an investor would expect to earn in an alternative investment with a similar risk profile
  - Represents the weighted average of the required return on the invested capital (customarily debt and equity) in a given company
- Weighted average cost of capital is simply a weighted average of the company's cost of debt (tax-effected) and cost of equity based on an assumed or "target" capital structure

Step III: Calculate Weighted Average Cost of Capital

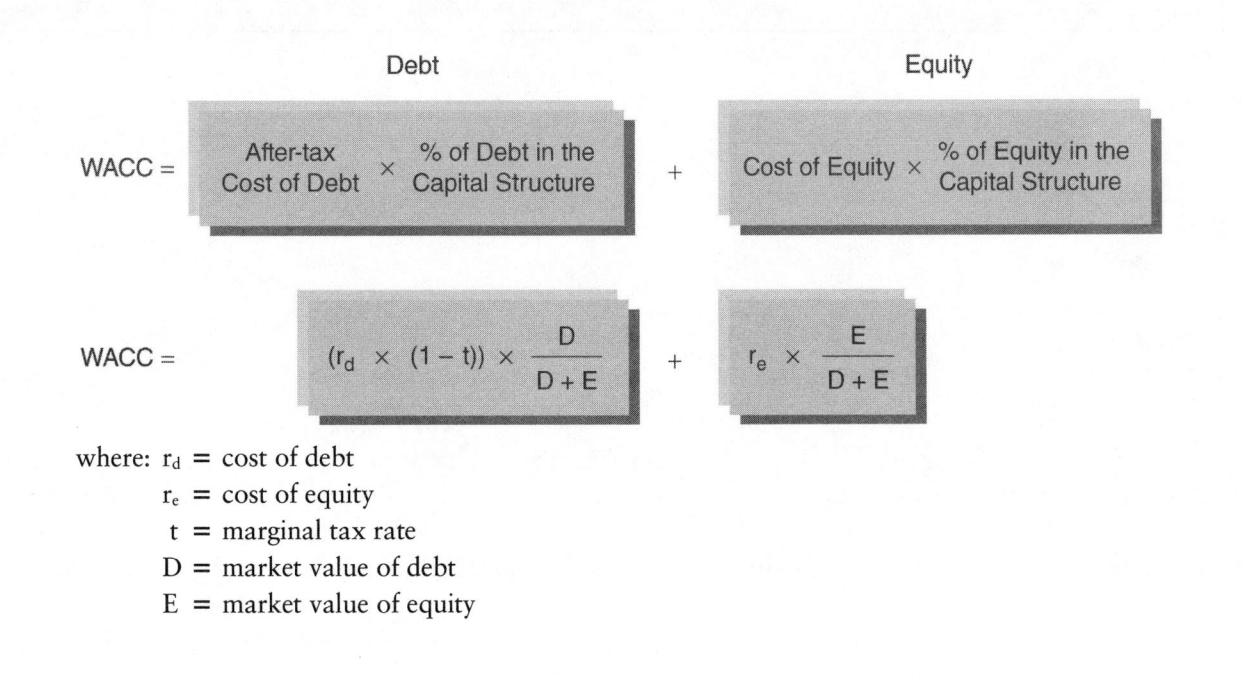

Debt   Equity

$$\text{WACC} = \left[\text{After-tax Cost of Debt} \times \text{\% of Debt in the Capital Structure} \right] + \left[\text{Cost of Equity} \times \text{\% of Equity in the Capital Structure} \right]$$

$$\text{WACC} = \left[(r_d \times (1 - t)) \times \frac{D}{D + E} \right] + \left[r_e \times \frac{E}{D + E} \right]$$

where: r_d = cost of debt

r_e = cost of equity

t = marginal tax rate

D = market value of debt

E = market value of equity

Step III: Calculate Weighted Average Cost of Capital

Steps for Calculating WACC

Step III(a): Determine Target Capital Structure

Step III(b): Estimate Cost of Debt (r_d)

Step III(c): Estimate Cost of Equity (r_e)

Step III(d): Calculate WACC

Step III: Calculate Weighted Average Cost of Capital

Step III(a): Determine Target Capital Structure

- WACC is predicated on choosing a target capital structure for the company that is consistent with long-term strategy
  - Target capital structure is represented by the debt-to-total capitalization (D/(D+E)) and equity-to-total capitalization (E/(D+E)) ratios
  - In the absence of explicit company guidance on target capital structure, examine the company's current and historical debt-to-total capitalization ratios as well as the capitalization of its peers
  - Public comparable companies provide a meaningful benchmark for target capital structure as it is assumed that their management teams are seeking to maximize shareholder value
- Approach used to determine a company's target capital structure may differ from firm to firm
  - For public companies, existing capital structure is generally used as the target capital structure as long as it is comfortably within the range of the comparables
  - For private companies, the mean or median for the comparables is typically used
  - Once the target capital structure is chosen, it is assumed to be held constant throughout the projection period

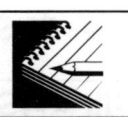

Step III: Calculate Weighted Average Cost of Capital

Step III(a): Determine Target Capital Structure (continued)

- Impact of capital structure on a company's WACC
  - When there is no debt in the capital structure, WACC is equal to the cost of equity
  - As the proportion of debt in the capital structure increases WACC gradually decreases due to the tax deductibility of interest expense
  - WACC continues to decrease up to the point where the optimal capital structure is reached
    - Once this threshold is surpassed, the cost of potential financial distress begins to override the tax advantages of debt
    - Both debt and equity investors demand a higher yield for their increased risk, thereby driving WACC upward beyond the optimal capital structure threshold

Step III: Calculate Weighted Average Cost of Capital

Step III(a): Determine Target Capital Structure (continued)

Optimal Capital Structure

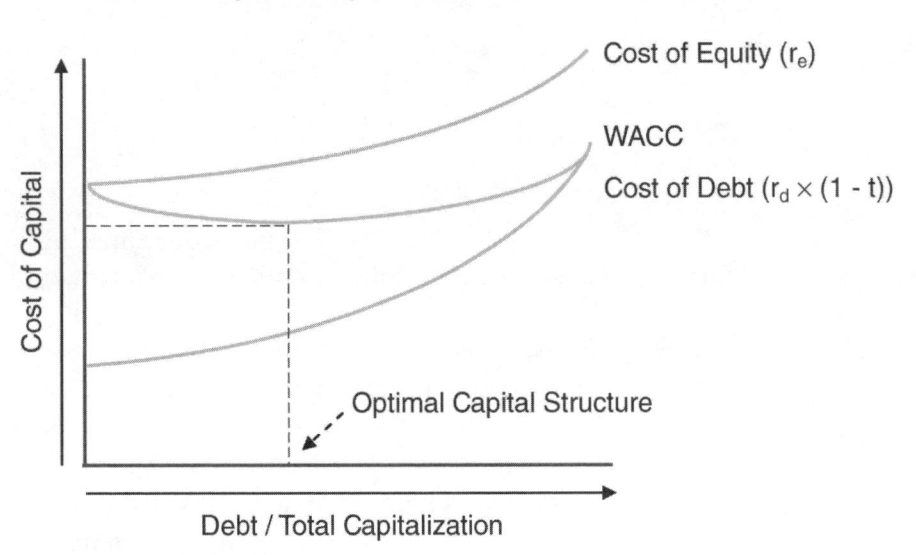

Step III: Calculate Weighted Average Cost of Capital

Step III(b): Estimate Cost of Debt (r_d)

- Company's cost of debt reflects its credit profile at the target capital structure
  - Based on a multitude of factors including size, sector, outlook, cyclicality, credit ratings, credit statistics, cash flow generation, financial policy, and acquisition strategy
  - In the event the company is not currently at its target capital structure, the cost of debt must be derived from peer companies
- Publicly traded bonds
  - Cost of debt is determined on the basis of the current yield on outstanding issues
- Private debt
  - Revolving credit facilities and term loans
  - Current yield on a company's outstanding debt serves as the best indicator of its expected cost of debt and reflects the risk of default

Step III: Calculate Weighted Average Cost of Capital

Step III(b): Estimate Cost of Debt (r_d) (continued)

- Absence of current market data (e.g., for companies with debt that is not actively traded)
  - Calculate the company's weighted average cost of debt on the basis of the at-issuance coupons of its current debt maturities
  - Not always accurate as it is backward-looking and may not reflect the company's cost of raising debt capital under prevailing market conditions
  - Preferred approach is to approximate a company's cost of debt based on its current (or implied) credit ratings at the target capital structure and the cost of debt for comparable credits
- Cost of debt is tax-effected at the company's marginal tax rate as interest payments are tax deductible

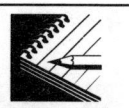

Step III: Calculate Weighted Average Cost of Capital

Step III(c): Estimate Cost of Equity (r_e)

- Cost of equity is the required annual rate of return that a company's equity investors expect to receive (including dividends)
  - Unlike the cost of debt, a company's cost of equity is not readily observable in the market
  - To calculate the expected return on a company's equity, typically employs a formula known as the capital asset pricing model (CAPM)
- Capital Asset Pricing Model (CAPM)
  - Based on the premise that equity investors need to be compensated for their assumption of systematic risk in the form of a risk premium, or the amount of market return in excess of a stated risk-free rate

Calculation of CAPM

Cost of Equity (r_e) = Risk-free Rate + Levered Beta × Market Risk Premium

Cost of Equity (r_e) = $r_f + \beta_L \times (r_m - r_f)$

where:
- r_f = risk-free rate
- β_L = levered beta
- r_m = expected return on the market
- $r_m - r_f$ = market risk premium

Step III: Calculate Weighted Average Cost of Capital

Step III(c): Estimate Cost of Equity (r_e) (continued)

- Risk-Free Rate (rf)
  - Risk free rate is the expected rate of return obtained by investing in a "riskless" security
    - U.S. government securities such as T-bills, T-notes, and T-bonds are accepted by the market as "risk-free" because they are backed by the full faith of the U.S. federal government
  - Investment banks may differ on accepted proxies for the appropriate risk-free rate
    - Yield on the 10-year U.S. Treasury note vs. yield on longer-term Treasuries
- Market Risk Premium (rm – rf or mrp)
  - Market risk premium is the spread of the expected market return over the risk-free rate
  - Ibbotson tracks data on the equity risk premium dating back to 1926
- Beta (β)
  - Beta is a measure of the covariance between the rate of return on a company's stock and the overall market return (systematic risk), with the S&P 500 traditionally used as a proxy for the market
  - As the S&P 500 has a beta of 1.0, a stock with a beta of 1.0 should have an expected return equal to that of the market

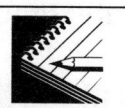

Step III: Calculate Weighted Average Cost of Capital

Step III(c): Estimate Cost of Equity (r_e) (continued)

- A stock with a beta of less than 1.0 has lower systematic risk than the market
- A stock with a beta greater than 1.0 has higher systematic risk
- This is captured in the CAPM, with a higher beta stock exhibiting a higher cost of equity and vice versa for lower beta stocks

- Unlevering Beta
  - Calculating WACC for a private company involves deriving beta from a group of publicly traded peer companies that may or may not have similar capital structures to one another or the target
    - To neutralize the effects of different capital structures (i.e., remove the influence of leverage), one must unlever the beta for each company in the peer group to achieve the asset beta ("unlevered beta")

Unlevering Beta

$$\beta_U = \frac{\beta_L}{\left(1 + \dfrac{D}{E} \times (1-t)\right)}$$

where
β_U = unlevered beta
β_L = levered beta
D/E = debt-to-equity ratio
t = marginal tax rate

Step III(c): Estimate Cost of Equity (r_e) (continued)

- Relevering Beta
  - After calculating the unlevered beta for each company, need to determine the average unlevered beta for the peer group
    - Average unlevered beta is then relevered using the company's target capital structure and marginal tax rate
    - Resulting levered beta serves as the beta for calculating the private company's cost of equity using the CAPM
    - For a public company that is not currently at its target capital structure, its asset beta must be calculated and then relevered at the target D/E

Relevering Beta

$$\beta_L = \beta_U \times \left(1 + \frac{D}{E} \times (1 - t)\right)$$

where: D/E = <u>target</u> debt-to-equity ratio

Step III: Calculate Weighted Average Cost of Capital

Step III(c): Estimate Cost of Equity (r_e) (continued)

- Size Premium (SP)
  - Concept is based on empirical evidence suggesting that smaller sized companies are riskier and, therefore, should have a higher cost of equity
    - Relies on the notion that smaller companies' risk is not entirely captured in their betas given limited trading volumes of their stock, making covariance calculations inexact
    - May choose to add a size premium to the CAPM formula for smaller companies to account for the perceived higher risk and, therefore, expected higher return

CAPM Formula Adjusted for Size Premium

$$r_e = r_f + \beta_L \times (r_m - r_f) + SP$$

where: SP = size premium

Step III: Calculate Weighted Average Cost of Capital

Step III(d): Calculate WACC

- Various components of Steps III(a) – III(c) are entered into the WACC formula

Debt   Equity

$$\text{WACC} = \boxed{\begin{array}{c}\text{After-tax} \\ \text{Cost of Debt}\end{array} \times \begin{array}{c}\text{\% of Debt in the} \\ \text{Capital Structure}\end{array}} \; + \; \boxed{\text{Cost of Equity} \times \begin{array}{c}\text{\% of Equity in the} \\ \text{Capital Structure}\end{array}}$$

$$\text{WACC} = \boxed{(r_d \times (1-t)) \times \frac{D}{D+E}} \; + \; \boxed{r_e \times \frac{E}{D+E}}$$

where: r_d = cost of debt
 r_e = cost of equity
 t = marginal tax rate
 D = market value of debt
 E = market value of equity

Step III: Calculate Weighted Average Cost of Capital

ValueCo Corporation
Weighted Average Cost of Capital Analysis
($ in millions)

WACC Calculation

Target Capital Structure

Debt-to-Total Capitalization	30.0%
Equity-to-Total Capitalization	70.0%

Cost of Debt

Cost-of-Debt	6.0%
Tax Rate	38.0%
After-tax Cost of Debt	**3.7%**

Cost of Equity

Risk-free Rate (1)	3.0%
Market Risk Premium (2)	6.62%
Levered Beta	1.29
Size Premium (3)	1.14%
Cost of Equity	**12.7%**

WACC	**10.0%**

Comparable Companies Unlevered Beta

Company	Predicted Levered Beta (4)	Market Value of Debt	Market Value of Equity	Debt/ Equity	Marginal Tax Rate	Unlevered Beta
BuyerCo	1.24	$2,200.0	$9,800.0	22.4%	38.0%	1.09
Sherman Co.	1.35	3,150.0	5,600.0	56.3%	38.0%	1.00
Gasparro Corp.	1.25	1,850.0	5,000.0	37.0%	38.0%	1.02
Goodson Corp	1.45	2,250.0	4,160.0	54.1%	38.0%	1.09
S. Momper & Co.	1.14	1,000.0	2,240.0	44.6%	38.0%	0.89
Mean	**1.29**			**42.9%**		**1.02**
Median	**1.25**			**44.6%**		**1.02**

ValueCo Relevered Beta

	Mean Unlevered Beta	Target Debt/ Equity	Target Marginal Tax Rate	Relevered Beta
Relevered Beta	1.02	42.9%	38.0%	**1.29**

WACC Sensitivity Analysis

		Pre-tax Cost of Debt				
		5.00%	5.50%	6.00%	6.50%	7.00%
Debt-to-Total Capitalization	10.0%	11.7%	11.8%	11.8%	11.8%	11.9%
	20.0%	10.8%	10.8%	10.9%	11.0%	11.0%
	30.0%	9.8%	9.9%	10.0%	10.1%	10.2%
	40.0%	8.9%	9.0%	9.1%	9.2%	9.4%
	50.0%	7.9%	8.1%	8.2%	8.4%	8.5%

(1) Interpolated yield on 20-year U.S. Treasury, sourced from *Bloomberg*
(2) Obtained from *Ibbotson SBBI Valuation Yearbook*
(3) Mid-Cap Decile size premium based on market capitalization, per Ibbotson
(4) Sourced from *Bloomberg*

Step IV: Determine Terminal Value

- DCF approach to valuation is based on determining the present value of all future FCF produced by a company
  - Infeasible to project a company's FCF indefinitely
- Use terminal value to capture the value of the company beyond the projection period
  - Typically calculated on the basis of the company's FCF (or a proxy such as EBITDA) in the final year of the projection period
- Terminal value typically accounts for a substantial portion of a company's value in a DCF
  - Important that the company's terminal year financial data represents a steady state level of financial performance
- There are two widely accepted methods used to calculate a company's terminal value – Exit Multiple Method (EMM) and Perpetuity Growth Method (PGM)

Step IV: Determine Terminal Value

Exit Multiple Method (EMM)

- Calculates the remaining value of a company's FCF produced after the projection period on the basis of a multiple of its terminal year EBITDA (or EBIT)
  - Multiple is typically based on the current LTM trading multiples for comparable companies
  - Important to use both a normalized trading multiple and EBITDA as current multiples may be affected by sector or economic cycles
  - Needs to be subjected to sensitivity analysis

Exit Multiple Method

$$\text{Terminal Value} = \text{EBITDA}_n \times \text{Exit Multiple}$$

where: n = terminal year of the projection period

Step IV: Determine Terminal Value

Perpetuity Growth Method (PGM)

- Calculates terminal value by treating a company's terminal year FCF as a perpetuity growing at an assumed rate
  - Method relies on the WACC calculation performed in Step III(c) and requires an assumption regarding the company's long-term, sustainable growth rate ("perpetuity growth rate")
  - Perpetuity growth rate is typically chosen on the basis of the company's expected long-term industry growth rate
  - Tends to be within a range of 2% to 4% (i.e., nominal GDP growth)

Perpetuity Growth Method

$$\text{Terminal Value} = \frac{FCF_n \times (1 + g)}{(r - g)}$$

where: FCF = unlevered free cash flow
        n = terminal year of the projection period
        g = perpetuity growth rate
        r = WACC

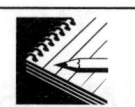

Step IV: Determine Terminal Value

Calculate Present Value

- Calculating present value centers on the notion that a dollar today is worth more than a dollar tomorrow
  - Concept known as the *time value of money*
  - Due to the fact that a dollar earns money through investments (capital appreciation) and/or interest (e.g., in a money market account)
  - In a DCF, a company's projected FCF and terminal value are discounted to the present at the company's WACC in accordance with the time value of money
- Present value calculation is performed by multiplying the FCF for each year in the projection period and the terminal value by its respective discount factor
  - Discount factor is fractional value representing present value of one dollar received at a future date given an assumed discount rate

Step IV: Determine Terminal Value

Calculate Present Value (continued)

Discount Factor

Discount Factor $= \dfrac{1}{(1 + \text{WACC})^n}$

$0.91 = \dfrac{\$1.00}{(1 + 10\%)^1}$

where: n = year in the projection period

Present Value Calculation Using a Year-End Discount Factor

PV of FCF_n = $\text{FCF}_n \times \text{Discount Factor}_n$

$91 million = $100 million $\times$ 0.91

Step IV: Determine Terminal Value

- Mid-Year Convention
  - To account for the fact that annual FCF is usually received throughout the year rather than at year-end
  - Use of a mid-year convention results in a slightly higher valuation than year-end discounting due to the fact that FCF is received sooner

Discount Factor Using a Mid-Year Convention

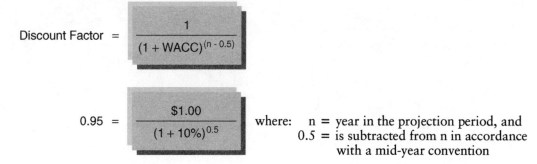

$$\text{Discount Factor} = \frac{1}{(1 + WACC)^{(n - 0.5)}}$$

$$0.95 = \frac{\$1.00}{(1 + 10\%)^{0.5}}$$

where: n = year in the projection period, and
0.5 = is subtracted from n in accordance with a mid-year convention

- Terminal Value Considerations
  - When employing mid-year convention for projection period, mid-year discounting is also applied for the terminal value under the PGM
  - EMM, which is typically based on the LTM trading multiples of comparable companies for a calendar year end EBITDA (or EBIT), uses year-end discounting

Step V: Calculate Present Value and Determine Valuation

Determine Valuation

- Calculate Enterprise Value
  - A company's projected FCF and terminal value are each discounted to the present and summed to provide an enterprise value

Enterprise Value Using Mid-Year Discounting

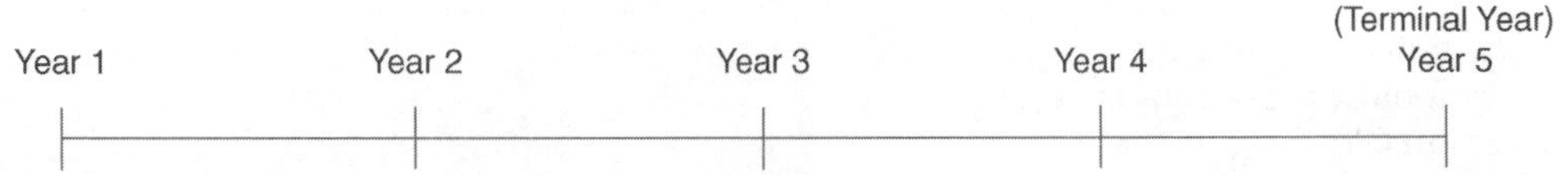

(Terminal Year)

| Year 1 | Year 2 | Year 3 | Year 4 | Year 5 |

$$\text{Enterprise Value} = \frac{FCF_1}{(1+WACC)^{0.5}} + \frac{FCF_2}{(1+WACC)^{1.5}} + \frac{FCF_3}{(1+WACC)^{2.5}} + \frac{FCF_4}{(1+WACC)^{3.5}} + \frac{FCF_5}{(1+WACC)^{4.5}}$$

$$+ \frac{(EBITDA_5 \times \text{Exit Multiple})}{(1+WACC)^{5}}$$

Step V: Calculate Present Value and Determine Valuation

Determine Valuation (continued)

- Derive Implied Equity Value
  - To derive implied equity value, the company's net debt, preferred stock, and noncontrolling interest are subtracted from the calculated enterprise value

$$\text{Implied Equity Value} = \text{Enterprise Value} - (\text{Net Debt} + \text{Preferred Stock} + \text{Noncontrolling Interest})$$

- Derive Implied Share Price
  - For publicly traded companies, implied equity value is divided by the company's fully diluted shares outstanding to calculate an implied share price

$$\text{Implied Share Price} = \frac{\text{Implied Equity Value}}{\text{Fully Diluted Shares Outstanding}}$$

Step V: Calculate Present Value and Determine Valuation

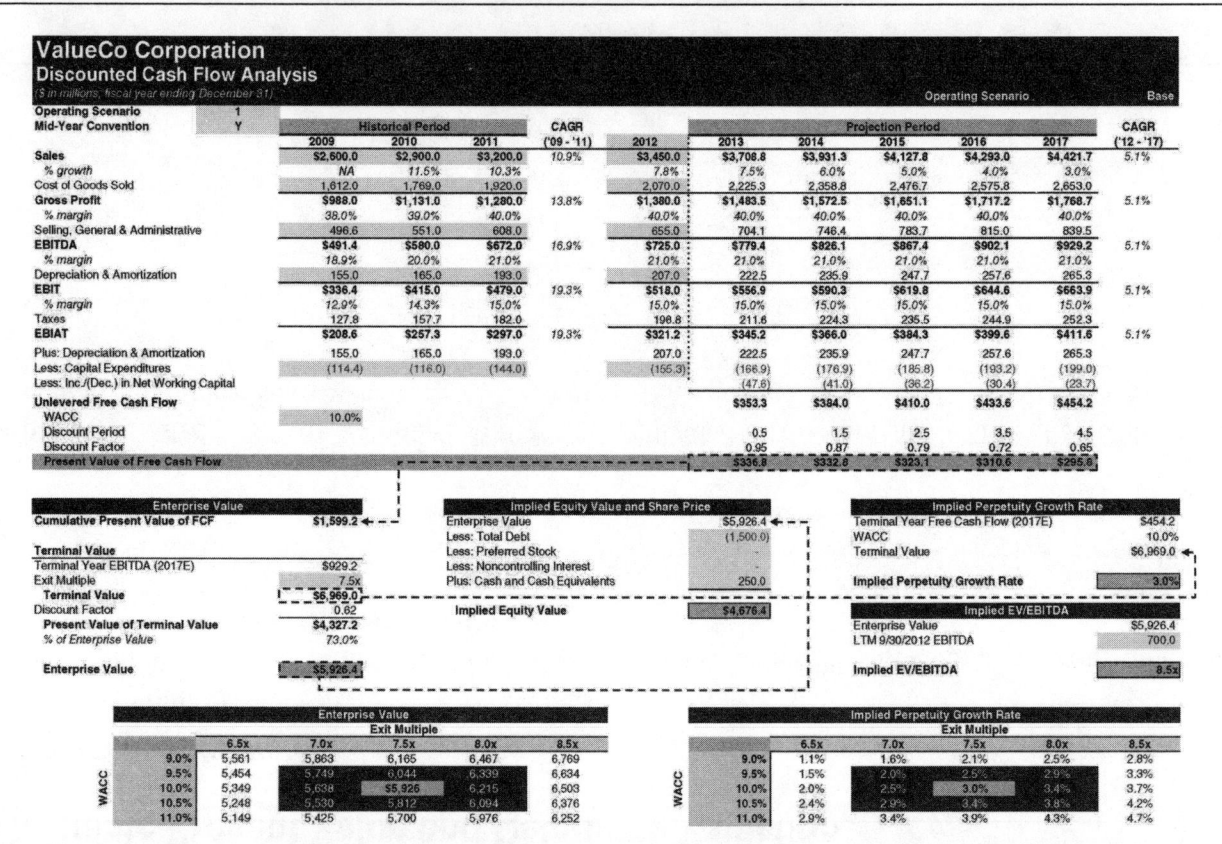

ValueCo Corporation
Discounted Cash Flow Analysis
($ in millions, fiscal year ending December 31)

Operating Scenario: Base

Operating Scenario: 1
Mid-Year Convention: Y

	Historical Period			CAGR ('09 - '11)	2012	Projection Period					CAGR ('12 - '17)
	2009	2010	2011			2013	2014	2015	2016	2017	
Sales	$2,500.0	$2,900.0	$3,200.0	10.9%	$3,450.0	$3,708.8	$3,931.3	$4,127.8	$4,293.0	$4,421.7	5.1%
% growth	NA	11.5%	10.3%		7.8%	7.5%	6.0%	5.0%	4.0%	3.0%	
Cost of Goods Sold	1,612.0	1,769.0	1,920.0		2,070.0	2,225.3	2,358.8	2,476.7	2,575.8	2,653.0	
Gross Profit	$988.0	$1,131.0	$1,280.0	13.8%	$1,380.0	$1,483.5	$1,572.5	$1,651.1	$1,717.2	$1,768.7	5.1%
% margin	38.0%	39.0%	40.0%		40.0%	40.0%	40.0%	40.0%	40.0%	40.0%	
Selling, General & Administrative	496.6	551.0	608.0		655.0	704.1	746.4	783.7	815.0	839.5	
EBITDA	$491.4	$580.0	$672.0	16.9%	$725.0	$779.4	$826.1	$867.4	$902.1	$929.2	5.1%
% margin	18.9%	20.0%	21.0%		21.0%	21.0%	21.0%	21.0%	21.0%	21.0%	
Depreciation & Amortization	155.0	165.0	193.0		207.0	222.5	235.9	247.7	257.6	265.3	
EBIT	$336.4	$415.0	$479.0	19.3%	$518.0	$556.9	$590.3	$619.8	$644.6	$663.9	5.1%
% margin	12.9%	14.3%	15.0%		15.0%	15.0%	15.0%	15.0%	15.0%	15.0%	
Taxes	127.8	157.7	182.0		198.8	211.6	224.3	235.5	244.9	252.3	
EBIAT	$208.6	$257.3	$297.0	19.3%	$321.2	$345.2	$366.0	$384.3	$399.6	$411.6	5.1%
Plus: Depreciation & Amortization	155.0	165.0	193.0		207.0	222.5	235.9	247.7	257.6	265.3	
Less: Capital Expenditures	(114.4)	(116.0)	(144.0)		(155.3)	(166.9)	(176.9)	(185.8)	(193.2)	(199.0)	
Less: Inc./(Dec.) in Net Working Capital						(47.6)	(41.0)	(36.2)	(30.4)	(23.7)	
Unlevered Free Cash Flow						$353.3	$384.0	$410.0	$433.6	$454.2	
WACC	10.0%										
Discount Period						0.5	1.5	2.5	3.5	4.5	
Discount Factor						0.95	0.87	0.79	0.72	0.65	
Present Value of Free Cash Flow						$336.8	$332.8	$323.1	$310.6	$295.6	

Enterprise Value

Cumulative Present Value of FCF	$1,599.2
Terminal Value	
Terminal Year EBITDA (2017E)	$929.2
Exit Multiple	7.5x
Terminal Value	$6,969.0
Discount Factor	0.62
Present Value of Terminal Value	$4,327.2
% of Enterprise Value	73.0%
Enterprise Value	$5,926.4

Implied Equity Value and Share Price

Enterprise Value	$5,926.4
Less: Total Debt	(1,500.0)
Less: Preferred Stock	-
Less: Noncontrolling Interest	-
Plus: Cash and Cash Equivalents	250.0
Implied Equity Value	$4,676.4

Implied Perpetuity Growth Rate

Terminal Year Free Cash Flow (2017E)	$454.2
WACC	10.0%
Terminal Value	$6,969.0
Implied Perpetuity Growth Rate	3.0%

Implied EV/EBITDA

Enterprise Value	$5,926.4
LTM 9/30/2012 EBITDA	700.0
Implied EV/EBITDA	8.5x

Enterprise Value

		Exit Multiple			
WACC	6.5x	7.0x	7.5x	8.0x	8.5x
9.0%	5,561	5,863	6,165	6,467	6,769
9.5%	5,454	5,749	6,044	6,339	6,634
10.0%	5,349	5,638	5,926	6,215	6,503
10.5%	5,248	5,530	5,812	6,094	6,376
11.0%	5,149	5,425	5,700	5,976	6,252

Implied Perpetuity Growth Rate

		Exit Multiple			
WACC	6.5x	7.0x	7.5x	8.0x	8.5x
9.0%	1.1%	1.6%	2.1%	2.5%	2.8%
9.5%	1.5%	2.0%	2.5%	2.9%	3.3%
10.0%	2.0%	2.5%	3.0%	3.4%	3.7%
10.5%	2.4%	2.9%	3.4%	3.8%	4.2%
11.0%	2.9%	3.4%	3.9%	4.3%	4.7%

Step V: Calculate Present Value and Determine Valuation

Perform Sensitivity Analysis

- DCF incorporates numerous assumptions, each of which can have a sizeable impact on valuation
  - Output is viewed in terms of a valuation range based on a series of key input assumptions, rather than as a single value
  - Exercise of deriving a valuation range by varying key inputs is called *sensitivity analysis*
- Key valuation drivers such as WACC, exit multiple, and perpetuity growth rate are the most commonly sensitized inputs in a DCF

Step V: Calculate Present Value and Determine Valuation

ValueCo Corporation
Sensitivity Analysis
($ in millions)

Enterprise Value

		Exit Multiple			
WACC		6.5x	7.0x	7.5x	8.0x	8.5x
9.0%	5,561	5,863	6,165	6,467	6,769
9.5%	5,454	5,749	6,044	6,339	6,634
10.0%	5,349	5,638	$5,926	6,215	6,503
10.5%	5,248	5,530	5,812	6,094	6,376
11.0%	5,149	5,425	5,700	5,976	6,252

Implied Equity Value

		Exit Multiple			
WACC		6.5x	7.0x	7.5x	8.0x	8.5x
9.0%	4,311	4,613	4,915	5,217	5,519
9.5%	4,204	4,499	4,794	5,089	5,384
10.0%	4,099	4,388	$4,676	4,965	5,253
10.5%	3,998	4,280	4,562	4,844	5,126
11.0%	3,899	4,175	4,450	4,726	5,002

Implied Perpetuity Growth Rate

		Exit Multiple			
WACC		6.5x	7.0x	7.5x	8.0x	8.5x
9.0%	1.1%	1.6%	2.1%	2.5%	2.8%
9.5%	1.5%	2.0%	2.5%	2.9%	3.3%
10.0%	2.0%	2.5%	3.0%	3.4%	3.7%
10.5%	2.4%	2.9%	3.4%	3.8%	4.2%
11.0%	2.9%	3.4%	3.9%	4.3%	4.7%

Implied Enterprise Value / LTM EBITDA

		Exit Multiple			
WACC		6.5x	7.0x	7.5x	8.0x	8.5x
9.0%	7.9x	8.4x	8.8x	9.2x	9.7x
9.5%	7.8x	8.2x	8.6x	9.1x	9.5x
10.0%	7.6x	8.1x	8.5x	8.9x	9.3x
10.5%	7.5x	7.9x	8.3x	8.7x	9.1x
11.0%	7.4x	7.7x	8.1x	8.5x	8.9x

PV of Terminal Value % of Enterprise Value

		Exit Multiple			
WACC		6.5x	7.0x	7.5x	8.0x	8.5x
9.0%	70.6%	72.1%	73.5%	74.7%	75.8%
9.5%	70.3%	71.9%	73.2%	74.5%	75.6%
10.0%	70.1%	71.6%	73.0%	74.3%	75.4%
10.5%	69.9%	71.4%	72.8%	74.0%	75.2%
11.0%	69.6%	71.2%	72.6%	73.8%	75.0%

Step V: Calculate Present Value and Determine Valuation

- Once a DCF range is determined, it should be compared to the valuation ranges derived from other methodologies
- Common missteps that can skew the DCF valuation include
  - Use of unrealistic financial projections (which generally has the largest impact), WACC assumptions, and/or Terminal value assumptions

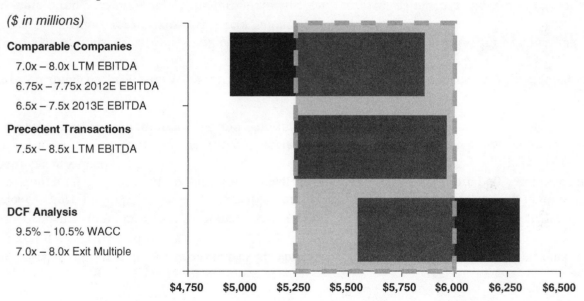

($ in millions)

Comparable Companies

7.0x – 8.0x LTM EBITDA

6.75x – 7.75x 2012E EBITDA

6.5x – 7.5x 2013E EBITDA

Precedent Transactions

7.5x – 8.5x LTM EBITDA

DCF Analysis

9.5% – 10.5% WACC

7.0x – 8.0x Exit Multiple

$4,750 $5,000 $5,250 $5,500 $5,750 $6,000 $6,250 $6,500

Key Pros and Cons

Pros

- **Cash flow-based** – reflects value of projected FCF, which represents a more fundamental approach to valuation than using multiples-based methodologies
- **Market independent** – more insulated from market aberrations such as bubbles and distressed periods
- **Self-sufficient** – does not rely on truly comparable companies or transactions, which may or may not exist, to frame valuation; a DCF is particularly important when there are limited or no "pure play" public comparables to the company being valued
- **Flexibility** – allows the banker to run multiple financial performance scenarios, including improving or declining growth rates, margins, capex requirements, and working capital efficiency

Cons

- **Dependence on financial projections** – accurate forecasting of financial performance is challenging, especially as the projection period lengthens
- **Sensitivity to assumptions** – relatively small changes in key assumptions, such as growth rates, margins, WACC, or exit multiple, can produce meaningfully different valuation ranges
- **Terminal value** – the present value of the terminal value can represent as much as three-quarters or more of the DCF valuation, which decreases the relevance of the projection period's annual FCF
- **Assumes constant capital structure** – basic DCF does not provide flexibility to change the company's capital structure over the projection period

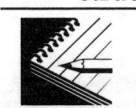

Chapter 4
Leveraged Buyouts

LBO Fundamentals

Key Participants

Characteristics of a Strong LBO Candidate

Economics of LBOs

Primary Exit / Monetization Strategies

LBO Financing: Structure

LBO Financing: Primary Sources

LBO Financing: Selected Key Terms

LBO Financing: Determining Financing Structure

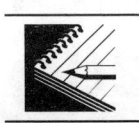

Overview of Leveraged Buyouts

- A leveraged buyout (LBO) is the acquisition of a company, division, business, or collection of assets ("target") using debt to finance a large portion of the purchase price
  - Remaining portion of the purchase price is funded with an equity contribution by a financial sponsor ("sponsor")
  - Sponsors have historically sought a 20%+ annualized return and an investment exit within five years
- In a traditional LBO, debt has typically comprised 60% to 70% of the financing structure, with equity comprising the remaining 30% to 40%
- Companies with stable and predictable cash flow, as well as substantial assets, generally represent attractive LBO candidates due to their ability to support larger quantities of debt
- Cash flow is used primarily to service and repay debt during the time from which the sponsor acquires the target until its exit ("investment horizon")
  - Debt repayment increases the equity portion of the capital structure
  - An appropriate LBO financing structure must balance the target's ability to service and repay debt
- Successful closing of an LBO relies upon sponsor's ability to obtain the requisite financing needed to acquire the target
- Debt used in an LBO is raised through the issuance of various types of loans, securities, and other instruments that are classified based on their security status as well as their seniority in the capital structure

Key Participants

> - Financial Sponsors
> - Investment Banks
> - Bank and Institutional Lenders
> - Bond Investors
> - Target Management

Financial Sponsors

- Term "financial sponsor" refers to traditional private equity (PE) firms, merchant banking divisions of investment banks, hedge funds, venture capital funds, and special purpose acquisition companies (SPACs)
- For PE firms, capital is organized into funds that are usually established as limited partnerships
- Sponsors vary greatly in terms of fund size, focus, and investment strategy
  - Size of a sponsor's fund(s), which can range from tens of millions to tens of billions of dollars (based on its ability to raise capital), dictate its investment parameters
  - Some firms specialize in specific sectors (such as industrials or media, for example) while others focus on specific situations (such as distressed companies/turnarounds, roll-ups, or corporate divestitures)
- Sponsor performs detailed due diligence on the target in evaluating an investment opportunity

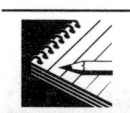

Key Participants

Investment Banks

- Investment banks play a key role in LBOs, both as a provider of financing and as a strategic M&A advisor
- Investment banks perform thorough due diligence on LBO targets (usually alongside their sponsor clients) and go through an extensive internal credit process in order to validate the target's business plan
- Following credit committee approval, the investment banks are able to provide a financing commitment to support the sponsor's bid
- For the bank debt, each arranger expects to hold a certain dollar amount of the revolving credit facility in its loan portfolio, while seeking to syndicate the remainder along with any term loan(s)

Key Participants

Bank and Institutional Lenders

- Bank and institutional lenders are the capital providers for the bank debt in an LBO financing structure
  - Traditional bank lenders provide capital for revolvers and amortizing term loans, while institutional lenders provide capital for longer tenored limited amortization term loans
  - Bank lenders typically consist of commercial banks, savings and loan institutions, finance companies, and the investment banks serving as arrangers
  - Institutional lender base is largely comprised of hedge funds, pension funds, prime funds, insurance companies, and structured vehicles
- Lenders perform due diligence and undergo an internal credit process before participating in an LBO financing
  - Also look to mitigate downside risk by requiring covenants and collateral coverage
- Prospective lenders attend a group meeting known as a "bank meeting"
  - Target's senior management team gives a detailed slideshow presentation about the company and its investment merits
  - Prospective lenders receive a hard copy of the presentation, as well as a confidential information memorandum (CIM)

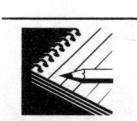

Key Participants

Bond Investors

- Bond investors are the purchasers of the high yield bonds issued as part of the LBO financing structure
  - Generally include high yield mutual funds, hedge funds, pension funds, insurance companies, and distressed debt funds
- Attend one-on-one meetings, known as "roadshow presentations"
  - Senior executives present the investment merits of the company and the proposed transaction
- Roadshow is typically a one- to two-week process
  - Bankers from the lead underwriting institution (and generally an individual from the sponsor team) accompany the target's management on meetings with potential investors
- Prior to the roadshow meeting, bond investors receive a preliminary offering memorandum (OM)
  - Legal document containing much of the target's business, industry, and financial information found in the bank book
  - Contains detailed information on the bonds, including a preliminary term sheet (excluding pricing) and a description of notes (DON)
  - Must satisfy a higher degree of legal scrutiny and disclosure (including risk factors)

Key Participants

Target Management

- Management plays a crucial role in the marketing of the target to potential buyers and lenders
  - Work closely with the bankers on the preparation of marketing materials and financial information
  - Serve as the primary face of the company and must articulate the investment merits of the transaction to constituents
  - Strong management team can create tangible value by driving favorable financing terms and pricing
- Typically holds a meaningful equity interest in the post-LBO company through "rolling" its existing equity or investing in the business alongside the sponsor at closing
  - Several layers of management typically also have the opportunity to participate (on a post-closing basis) in a stock option-based compensation package, generally tied to an agreed upon set of financial targets of the company
- LBO originated and led by a target's existing management team is referred to as a management buyout (MBO)
  - Basic premise behind an MBO is that the management team believes it can create more value running the company on its own than under current ownership
  - Structure also serves to eliminate the conflict between management and the board of directors/shareholders
  - May be motivated by the belief that the market is undervaluing the company

Characteristics of a Strong LBO Candidate

- Financial sponsors as a group are highly flexible investors that seek attractive investment opportunities across a broad range of sectors, geographies, and situations
- Certain common traits emerge among traditional LBO candidates

> - Strong Cash Flow Generation
> - Leading and Defensible Market Positions
> - Growth Opportunities
> - Efficiency Enhancement Opportunities
> - Low Capex Requirements
> - Strong Asset Base
> - Proven Management Team

- For a publicly traded LBO candidate, a sponsor may perceive the target as undervalued by the market or recognize opportunities for growth and efficiency not being exploited by current management
- Target only represents an attractive LBO opportunity if it can be purchased at a price and utilizing a financing structure that provides sufficient returns with a viable exit strategy

Characteristics of a Strong LBO Candidate

Strong Cash Flow Generation

- Ability to generate strong, predictable cash flow is critical for LBO candidates given highly leveraged capital structure
- Debt investors require a business model that demonstrates the ability to support periodic interest payments and debt repayment
- Business characteristics that support the predictability of robust cash flow increase a company's attractiveness as an LBO candidate
- Prospective buyers and financing providers seek to confirm a given LBO candidate's cash flow generation during due diligence to gain the requisite level of comfort with the target management's projections
- Cash flow projections are usually stress-tested (sensitized) based on historical volatility and potential future business and economic conditions to ensure the ability to support the LBO financing structure under challenging circumstances

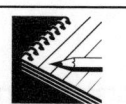

Characteristics of a Strong LBO Candidate

Leading and Defensible Market Positions

- Leading and defensible market positions generally reflect entrenched customer relationships, brand name recognition, superior products and services, a favorable cost structure, and scale advantages, among other attributes
- Create barriers to entry and increase the stability and predictability of a company's cash flow
- Sponsor spends a great deal of time during due diligence seeking assurance that the target's market positions are secure (and can potentially be expanded)
- Depending on the sponsor's familiarity with the sector, consultants may be hired to perform independent studies analyzing market share and barriers to entry

Growth Opportunities

- Sponsors seek companies with growth potential, both organically and through potential future bolt-on acquisitions
- Profitable top line growth at above-market rates helps drive outsized returns, generating greater cash available for debt repayment while also increasing EBITDA and enterprise value
- Companies with robust growth profiles have a greater likelihood of driving EBITDA "multiple expansion" during the sponsor's investment horizon
- Larger companies tend to benefit from their scale, market share, purchasing power, and lower risk profile
- In some cases, the sponsor opts not to maximize the amount of debt financing at purchase

Characteristics of a Strong LBO Candidate

Efficiency Enhancement Opportunities

- Sponsors seek opportunities to improve operational efficiencies and generate cost savings
- Traditional cost-saving measures include lowering corporate overhead, streamlining operations, reducing headcount, rationalizing the supply chain, and implementing new management information systems
- Sponsors must be careful not to jeopardize existing sales or attractive growth opportunities
- Extensive cuts in marketing, capex, or research & development, for example, may hurt customer retention, new product development, or other growth initiatives

Low Capex Requirements

- All else being equal, low capex requirements enhance a company's cash flow generation capabilities
- Best LBO candidates tend to have limited capital investment needs
- During due diligence, the sponsor and its advisors focus on differentiating those expenditures deemed necessary to continue operating the business ("maintenance capex") from those that are discretionary ("growth capex")

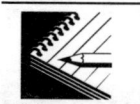

Characteristics of a Strong LBO Candidate

Strong Asset Base

- Strong asset base pledged as collateral against a loan benefits lenders by increasing the likelihood of principal recovery in the event of bankruptcy (and liquidation)
- Target's asset base is particularly important in the leveraged loan market, where the value of the assets helps dictate the amount of bank debt available
- Strong asset base also tends to signify high barriers to entry because of the substantial capital investment required
- Company with little or no assets can still be an attractive LBO candidate provided it generates sufficient cash flow

Proven Management Team

- Proven management team serves to increase the attractiveness (and value) of an LBO candidate
- Talented management is critical in an LBO scenario given the need to operate under a highly leveraged capital structure with ambitious performance targets
- For LBO candidates with strong management, the sponsor usually seeks to keep the existing team in place post-acquisition
- Instances where the target's management is weak, sponsors seek to add value by making key changes to the existing team or installing a new team altogether to run the company

Economics of LBOs

Returns Analysis – Internal Rate of Return

- Internal rate of return (IRR) is the primary metric by which sponsors gauge the attractiveness of a potential LBO
- IRR measures the total return on a sponsor's equity investment, including any additional equity contributions made, or dividends received, during the investment horizon
- IRR is defined as the discount rate that must be applied to the sponsor's cash outflows and inflows during the investment horizon in order to produce a net present value (NPV) of zero

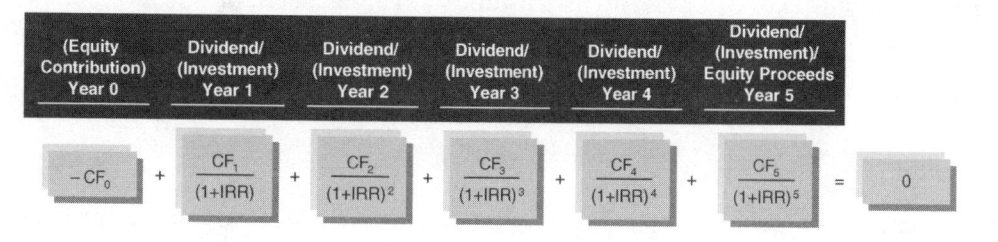

(Equity Contribution) Year 0	Dividend/ (Investment) Year 1	Dividend/ (Investment) Year 2	Dividend/ (Investment) Year 3	Dividend/ (Investment) Year 4	Dividend/ (Investment)/ Equity Proceeds Year 5

$$-CF_0 + \frac{CF_1}{(1+IRR)} + \frac{CF_2}{(1+IRR)^2} + \frac{CF_3}{(1+IRR)^3} + \frac{CF_4}{(1+IRR)^4} + \frac{CF_5}{(1+IRR)^5} = 0$$

- Comfort with meeting acceptable IRR thresholds is critical – with a 20%+ threshold serving as a "rule of thumb"
- Primary IRR drivers include the target's projected financial performance, purchase price, and financing structure (particularly the size of the equity contribution), as well as the exit multiple and year
- Sponsor seeks to minimize the price paid and equity contribution while gaining a strong degree of confidence in the target's future financial performance and the ability to exit at a sufficient valuation

Economics of LBOs

Returns Analysis – Cash Return

- Sponsors also examine returns on the basis of a multiple of their cash investment ("cash return")
  - Assuming a sponsor contributes $300 million of equity and receives equity proceeds of $1,000 million at the end of the investment horizon, the cash return is 3.3x (assuming no additional investments or dividends during the period)
  - Cash return approach does not factor in the time value of money

How LBOs Generate Returns

- LBOs generate returns through a combination of debt repayment and growth in enterprise value

How Leverage is Used to Enhance Returns

- Assuming a fixed enterprise value at exit, using a higher percentage of debt in the financing structure (and a correspondingly smaller equity contribution) generates higher returns
- Higher level of debt provides the additional benefit of greater tax savings realized due to the tax deductibility of a higher amount of interest expense
- While increased leverage may be used to generate enhanced returns, there are certain clear trade-offs
  - Higher leverage increases the company's risk profile (and probability of financial distress), limiting financial flexibility and making the company more susceptible to business or economic downturns

Primary Exit / Monetization Strategies

- Sponsors aim to exit or monetize their investments within a five-year holding period in order to provide timely returns to their limited partners (LPs)
  - Returns typically realized via a sale to another company (commonly referred to as "strategic sale"), sale to another sponsor, or an IPO
  - Sponsors may also extract a return prior to exit through a dividend recapitalization or a below par debt repurchase
- Sponsor ideally has increased the target's EBITDA (e.g., through organic growth, acquisitions, and/or increased profitability) and reduced its debt by the end of the investment horizon
- Sponsor also seeks to achieve multiple expansion upon exit
- Several strategies aimed at achieving a higher exit multiple
  - Increase the target's size and scale
  - Meaningful operational improvements
  - Repositioning of the business toward more highly valued industry segments
  - Acceleration of the target's organic growth rate and/or profitability
  - Accurate timing of a cyclical or economic upturn

Primary Exit / Monetization Strategies

Primary LBO exit/monetization strategies for financial sponsors

Sale of Business	■ Traditionally, sponsors have sought to sell portfolio companies to strategic buyers ■ Typically strongest potential bidder due to their ability to realize synergies from the target and, therefore, pay a higher price
Initial Public Offering	■ Sponsor sells a portion of its shares in the target to the public ■ Post-IPO, the sponsor typically retains the largest single equity stake in the target with the understanding that a full exit will come through future follow-on equity offerings or an eventual sale of the company
Dividend Recapitalization	■ Target raises proceeds through the issuance of additional debt to pay shareholders a dividend ■ Provides the sponsor with a viable option for monetizing a sizeable portion of its investment prior to exit
Below Par Debt Repurchase	■ Private equity firms have the flexibility to purchase the bank debt and high yield securities of their portfolio companies ■ Particularly attractive when debt can be bought at distressed levels

LBO Financing: Structure

- In a traditional LBO, debt has typically comprised 60% to 70% of the financing structure
- Given the inherently high leverage associated with an LBO, the various debt components of the capital structure are usually deemed non-investment grade
  - Rated 'Ba1' and below by Moody's Investor Service and 'BB+' and below by Standard and Poor's
- Debt portion of the LBO financing structure may include a broad array of loans, securities, or other debt instruments with varying terms and conditions that appeal to different classes of investors
- The higher a given debt instrument ranks in the capital structure hierarchy, the lower its risk and, consequently, the lower its cost of capital to the borrower/issuer
  - Cost of capital tends to be inversely related to the flexibility permitted by the applicable debt instrument
  - For example, bank debt usually represents the least expensive form of LBO financing

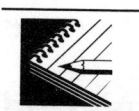

LBO Financing: Structure

General Ranking of Financing Sources in an LBO Capital Structure

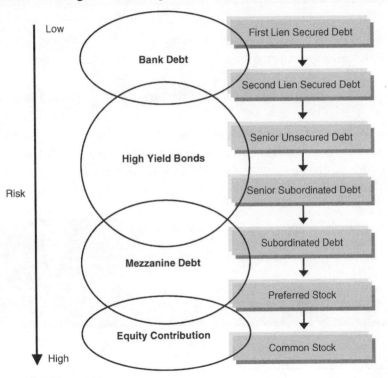

LBO Financing: Primary Sources

Bank Debt

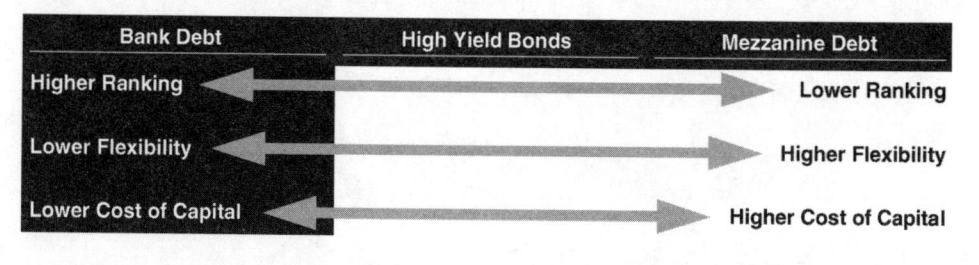

Bank Debt	High Yield Bonds	Mezzanine Debt
Higher Ranking		Lower Ranking
Lower Flexibility		Higher Flexibility
Lower Cost of Capital		Higher Cost of Capital

- Bank debt is an integral part of the LBO financing structure, consistently serving as a substantial source of capital
- Typically comprised of a revolving credit facility (which may be borrowed, repaid, and reborrowed) and one or more term loan (TL) tranches (which may not be reborrowed once repaid)
- Revolving credit facility may take the form of a traditional "cash flow" revolver or an asset based lending (ABL) facility
- Bank debt is issued in the private market and is therefore not subject to SEC regulations and disclosure requirements
- Typically bears interest (payable on a quarterly basis) at a given benchmark rate, usually LIBOR or the Base Rate, plus an applicable margin ("spread") based on the credit of the borrower

LBO Financing: Primary Sources

High Yield Bonds

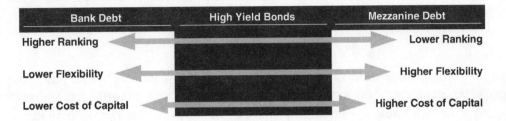

- High yield bonds are non-investment grade debt securities that obligate the issuer to make interest payments to bondholders at regularly defined intervals (typically on a semiannual basis) and repay principal at a stated maturity date, usually seven to ten years after issuance
- As opposed to term loans, high yield bonds are non-amortizing with entire principal due as bullet payment at maturity
- Due to their junior, typically unsecured position in the capital structure, longer maturities, and less restrictive incurrence covenants (as set forth in an indenture), high yield bonds feature a higher coupon than bank debt to compensate investors for the greater risk
- Typically pay interest at a fixed rate, which is priced at issuance on the basis of a spread to a benchmark Treasury
- While high yield bonds may be structured with a floating rate coupon, this is not common for LBO financings
- High yield bonds enable sponsors to substantially increase leverage levels beyond those available in the leveraged loan market alone

LBO Financing: Primary Sources

Mezzanine Debt

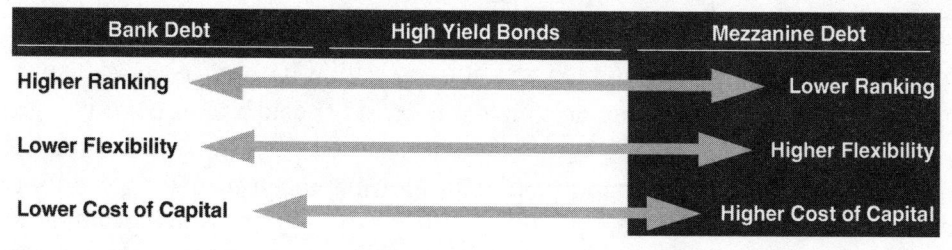

- Mezzanine debt refers to a layer of capital that lies between traditional debt and equity
- Highly negotiated instrument between the issuer and investors that is tailored to meet the financing needs of the specific transaction and required investor returns
- Typical investors include dedicated mezzanine funds and hedge funds
- Maturities for mezzanine debt, like terms, vary substantially, but tend to be similar to those for high yield bonds
- For sponsors, mezzanine debt provides incremental capital at a cost below that of equity, which enables them to stretch leverage levels and purchase price when alternative capital sources are inaccessible

LBO Financing: Primary Sources

Equity Contribution

- Remaining portion of LBO funding comes in the form of an equity contribution by the financial sponsor and rolled/contributed equity by the target's management
  - Typically ranges from approximately 30% to 40% of the LBO financing structure
- For large LBOs, several sponsors may team up to create a consortium of buyers, thereby reducing the amount of each individual sponsor's equity contribution (known as a "club deal")
- Equity contribution provides a cushion for lenders and bondholders in the event that the company's enterprise value deteriorates as equity value is eliminated before debt holders lose recovery value
- Rollover/contributed equity by existing company management and/or key shareholders varies according to the situation, but often ranges from approximately 2% to 5% (or more) of the overall equity portion

LBO Financing: Selected Key Terms

- Within and across the broad categories of debt instruments used in LBO financings there are a number of key terms that affect risk, cost, flexibility, and investor base

Summary of Selected Key Terms

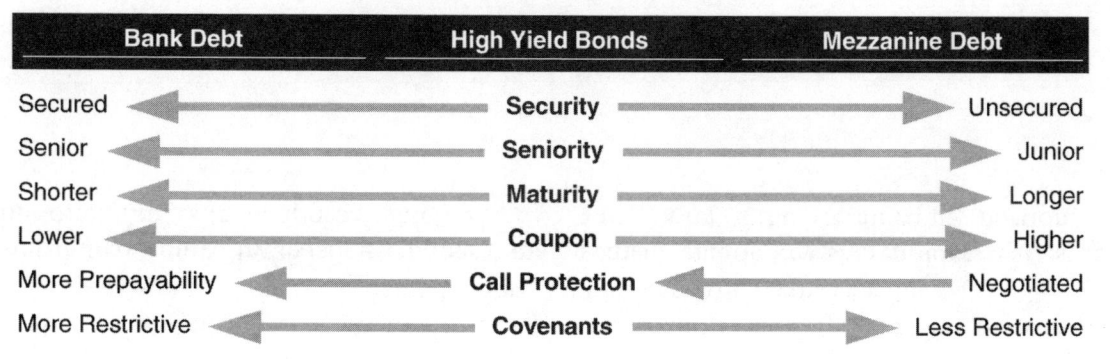

Bank Debt	High Yield Bonds	Mezzanine Debt
Secured	Security	Unsecured
Senior	Seniority	Junior
Shorter	Maturity	Longer
Lower	Coupon	Higher
More Prepayability	Call Protection	Negotiated
More Restrictive	Covenants	Less Restrictive

LBO Financing: Selected Key Terms

Security

- Security refers to the pledge of, or lien on, collateral that is granted by the borrower to the holders of a given debt instrument
- Collateral represents assets, property, and/or securities pledged by a borrower to secure a loan or other debt obligation, which is subject to seizure and/or liquidation in the event of a default
- Depending upon the volatility of the target's cash flow, creditors may require higher levels of collateral coverage as protection

LBO Financing: Selected Key Terms

Seniority

- Seniority refers to priority status of a creditor's claims against the borrower/issuer relative to those of other creditors
- Achieved through either *contractual* or *structural* subordination
- **Contractual Subordination**
  - Refers to the priority status of debt instruments at the same legal entity
  - Established through subordination provisions in an indenture, which stipulate that the claims of senior creditors must be satisfied in full before those of junior creditors (generally "senior" status is limited to bank lenders or similar creditors, not trade creditors)

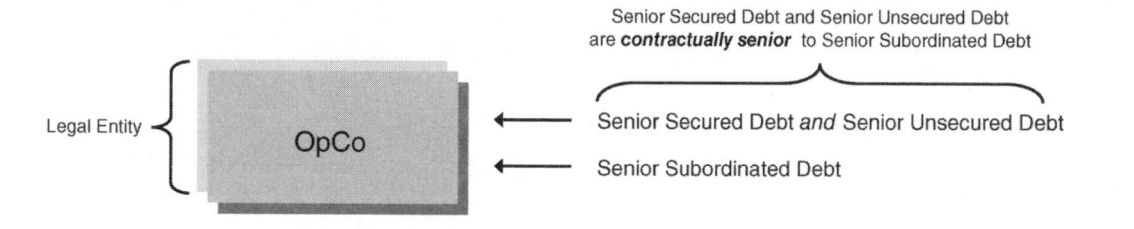

Seniority (continued)

- **Structural Subordination**
  - Refers to the priority status of debt instruments at different legal entities within a company
    - For example, debt obligations at OpCo, where the company's assets are located, are structurally senior to debt obligations at HoldCo so long as such HoldCo obligations do not benefit from a guarantee (credit support) from OpCo

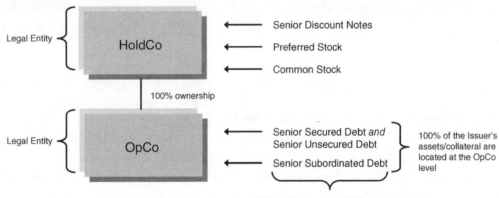

LBO Financing: Selected Key Terms

Maturity

- The maturity ("tenor" or "term") of a debt obligation refers to the length of time the instrument remains outstanding until the full principal amount must be repaid
- Shorter tenor debt is deemed less risky than debt with longer maturities as it is required to be repaid earlier
    - All else being equal, shorter tenor debt carries a lower cost of capital than longer tenor debt of the same credit
- In an LBO, various debt instruments with different maturities are issued to finance the debt portion of the transaction
    - Bank debt tends to have shorter maturities, often five to six years for revolvers and seven (or sometimes seven and one-half years) for institutional term loans
    - Historically, high yield bonds have had a maturity of seven to ten years

Coupon

- Coupon refers to the annual interest rate ("pricing") paid on a debt obligation's principal amount outstanding
- Bank debt generally pays interest on a quarterly basis, while bonds generally pay interest on a semiannual basis
- There are a number of factors that affect a debt obligation's coupon, including the type of debt (and its investor class), ratings, security, seniority, maturity, covenants, and prevailing market conditions
- In a traditional LBO financing structure, bank debt tends to be the lowest cost of capital debt instrument because it has higher facility rating, first lien security, higher seniority, a shorter maturity, and more restrictive covenants than high yield bonds

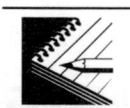

LBO Financing: Selected Key Terms

Call Protection

- Call protection refers to certain restrictions on voluntary prepayments (of bank debt) or redemptions (of bonds) during a defined time period within a given debt instrument's term
- Standard for high yield bonds
  - Typically set at four years ("Non call-4" or "NC-4") for a seven/eight-year fixed rate bond and five years ("NC-5") for a ten-year fixed rate bond
  - Redemption of bonds prior to maturity requires the issuer to pay a premium in accordance with a defined call schedule as set forth in an indenture, which dictates call prices for set dates

Call Schedules

8-year, 8% Notes due 2020, NC-4			10-year, 10% Notes due 2022, NC-5		
Year	Formula	Call Price	Year	Formula	Call Price
2012 - 2015	Non-callable		2012 - 2015	Non-callable	
2016	Par plus 1/2 the coupon	$104.000	2016	Non-callable	
2017	Par plus 1/4 the coupon	$102.000	2017	Par plus 1/2 the coupon	$105.000
2018 +	Par	$100.000	2018	Par plus 1/3 the coupon	$103.333
-	-	-	2019	Par plus 1/6 the coupon	$101.667
-	-	-	2020 +	Par	$100.000

- Traditional first lien bank debt has no call protection, meaning that the borrower can repay principal at any time without penalty

LBO Financing: Selected Key Terms

Covenants

- Covenants are provisions in credit agreements and indentures intended to protect against the deterioration of the borrower/issuer's credit quality
  - Govern specific actions that may or may not be taken during the term of the debt obligation
  - Failure to comply with a covenant may trigger an event of default
- While many of the covenants in credit agreements and indentures are similar in nature, a key difference is that traditional bank debt features financial *maintenance* covenants while high yield bonds have less restrictive *incurrence* covenants
  - Financial *maintenance* covenants require the borrower to "maintain" a certain credit profile at all times through compliance with certain financial ratios or tests on a quarterly basis
- **Bank Debt Covenants**
  - Typical credit agreement contains two to three *maintenance* covenants
  - Required maintenance leverage ratios typically decrease ("step down") throughout the term of the loan
  - Similarly, the coverage ratios typically increase over time

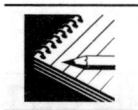

Covenants (continued)

- **High Yield Bond Covenants**
  - Many of the covenants found in a high yield bond indenture are similar to those found in a bank debt credit agreement
  - Key difference is that indentures contain *incurrence* covenants as opposed to *maintenance* covenants
  - *Incurrence* covenants only prevent issuer from taking specific actions (e.g., incurring additional debt, paying dividends) in the event it is not in pro forma compliance with a "Ratio Test"
  - Ratio Test – often a coverage test (e.g., fixed charge coverage ratio), although it may also be structured as a leverage test (e.g., total debt-to-EBITDA)

LBO Financing: Determining Financing Structure

- As with valuation, determining the appropriate LBO financing structure involves a mix of art and science
  - This structuring exercise centers on fundamental company-specific cash flow, returns, and credit statistics analysis, as well as examining market conditions and precedent LBO deals
- Ultimate LBO financing structure must balance the needs of the financial sponsor, debt investors, the company, and management, which are not necessarily aligned
  - Sponsor often seeks to maximize leverage so as to generate the highest IRR
  - Lenders and bondholders, on the other hand, have an interest in limiting leverage as well as introducing covenants and other provisions to protect their principal
  - Company's best interests often reside with more moderate leverage from both a risk management and growth perspective
  - Management is often both a meaningful shareholder aligned with the sponsor in the pursuit of maximum IRRs, as well as a caretaker of the company focused on mitigating risk and preserving flexibility
- Structuring an LBO is predicated on analyzing the target's cash flows and credit statistics, including leverage and coverage ratios
  - Analysis centers on crafting a financing structure that provides high leverage while maintaining sufficient cushion and room to maneuver in a downside scenario
- Target's sector plays a key role in determining the appropriate LBO structure, as reflected in total leverage, bank debt/high yield bond mix, and terms of the debt

LBO Financing: Determining Financing Structure

- As with comparable companies and precedent transactions for valuation multiples, prevailing market conditions and precedent LBO deals play a critical role in determining leverage multiples and key financing terms
- Leveraged finance professionals analyze recent LBO transactions to help determine what the market will bear in terms of financing structures for new deals
  - Recent LBOs in the target's sector are most relevant as well as deals of similar size and rating
- Current market conditions for bank debt and high yield bonds need to be closely monitored throughout the LBO process, especially as the commitment letters are finalized
- Leveraged finance markets can be volatile with "market-clearing" terms often changing quickly, potentially rendering recent precedents meaningless
- There are clear market windows where issuers are able to take advantage of strong market conditions interspersed with more challenging periods
- At a given point in time, investment banking professionals look at new issue volumes, trading levels by ratings categories, and trading levels for comparable debt securities to determine the state of the markets
  - Once the initial financing structure is determined, it is run through the LBO model and sensitized to analyze IRRs and pro forma credit metrics

Chapter 5
LBO Analysis

Overview of LBO Analysis

- Core analytical tool used to assess financing structure, investment returns, and valuation in leveraged buyout scenarios
- Same techniques can also be used to assess refinancing opportunities and restructuring alternatives for corporate issuers
- Requires specialized knowledge of financial modeling, leveraged debt capital markets, M&A, and accounting
- At the center of an LBO analysis is a financial model (the "LBO model")
  - Constructed with the flexibility to analyze a given target's performance under multiple financing structures and operating scenarios

Financing Structure

- On the debt financing side, the banker uses LBO analysis to help craft a viable financing structure for the target, which encompasses the amount and type of debt, as well as an equity contribution from a financial sponsor
- The analysis of an LBO financing structure is typically spearheaded by an investment bank's leveraged finance and capital market teams
- Once the private equity buyer chooses the preferred financing structure, the deal team presents it to the bank's internal credit committee(s) for approval
- Following committee approval, the investment banks typically provide a financing commitment, which is then submitted to the seller and its advisor(s) as part of its final bid package

Overview of LBO Analysis

Valuation

- LBO analysis is used by sponsors, bankers, and other finance professionals to determine an implied valuation range for a given target in a potential LBO sale based on achieving acceptable returns
- Valuation output is premised on key variables such as financial projections, purchase price, and financing structure, as well as exit multiple and year
- In an M&A sell-side advisory context, the banker conducts LBO analysis to assess valuation from the perspective of a financial sponsor
  - Similarly, on buy-side engagements, the banker typically performs LBO analysis to help determine a purchase price range for the target
  - For a strategic buyer, this analysis is used to frame valuation and bidding strategy by analyzing the price that a competing sponsor bidder might be willing to pay for the target

LBO Analysis Steps

Step I. Locate and Analyze the Necessary Information

Step II. Build the Pre-LBO Model

a. Build Historical and Projected Income Statement through EBIT
b. Input Opening Balance Sheet and Project Balance Sheet Items
c. Build Cash Flow Statement through Investing Activities

Step III. Input Transaction Structure

a. Enter Purchase Price Assumptions
b. Enter Financing Structure into Sources and Uses
c. Link Sources and Uses to Balance Sheet Adjustments Columns

Step IV. Complete the Post-LBO Model

   a. Build Debt Schedule
   b. Complete Pro Forma Income Statement from EBIT to Net Income
   c. Complete Pro Forma Balance Sheet
   d. Complete Pro Forma Cash Flow Statement

Step V. Perform LBO Analysis

   a. Analyze Financing Structure
   b. Perform Returns Analysis
   c. Determine Valuation
   d. Create Transaction Summary Page

Step I: Locate and Analyze the Necessary Information

- When performing LBO analysis, the first step is to collect, organize, and analyze all available information on the target, its sector, and the specifics of the transaction
- In an organized sale process, the sell-side advisor provides such detail to prospective buyers, including financial projections that usually form the basis for the initial LBO model
  - This information is typically contained in a CIM, with additional information provided via a management presentation and data room
- In the absence of a CIM or supplemental company information (e.g., if the target is not being actively sold), the banker must rely upon public sources to perform preliminary due diligence and develop an initial set of financial projections
- Regardless of whether there is a formal sale process, it is important for the banker to independently verify as much information as possible about the target and its sector

Step II: Build the Pre-LBO Model

Step II(a): Build Historical and Projected Income Statement through EBIT

Step II(b): Input Opening Balance Sheet and Project Balance Sheet Items

Step II(c): Build Cash Flow Statement through Investing Activities

Step II: Build the Pre-LBO Model

Step II(a): Build Historical and Projected Income Statement through EBIT

- Typically begin the pre-LBO model by inputting the target's historical income statement information for the prior three-year period, if available
- Historical income statement is generally only built through EBIT, as the target's prior annual interest expense and net income are not relevant given that the target will be recapitalized through the LBO
- Management projections for sales through EBIT, as provided in the CIM, are then entered into an assumptions page which feeds into the projected income statement until other operating scenarios are developed/provided

Additional Cases

- In addition to the Management Case, the deal team typically develops its own, more conservative operating scenario, known as the "Base Case"
- Base Case is generally premised on management assumptions, but with adjustments made based on the deal team's independent due diligence, research, and perspectives
- The bank's internal credit committee(s) also requires the deal team to analyze the target's performance under one or more stress cases in order to gain comfort with the target's ability to service and repay debt during periods of duress
  - "Downside Cases" typically present the target's financial performance with haircuts to top line growth, margins, and potentially capex and working capital efficiency
- The operating scenario that the deal team ultimately uses to set covenants and market the transaction to investors is provided by the sponsor (the "Sponsor Case")

Step II: Build the Pre-LBO Model

Step II(b): Input Opening Balance Sheet and Project Balance Sheet Items

- The opening balance sheet (and potentially projected balance sheet data) for the target is typically provided in the CIM and entered into the pre-LBO model
- In addition to the traditional balance sheet accounts, new line items necessary for modeling the pro forma LBO financing structure are added, such as financing fees (which are amortized) under long-term assets and detailed line items for the new financing structure under long-term liabilities
- Must then build functionality into the model in order to input the new LBO financing structure
  - Accomplished by inserting "adjustment" columns to account for the additions and subtractions to the opening balance sheet that result from the LBO
- Also insert a "pro forma" column, which nets the adjustments made to the opening balance sheet and serves as the starting point for projecting the target's post-LBO balance sheet throughout the projection period
- Inputs for the adjustment columns, which bridge from the opening balance sheet to the pro forma closing balance sheet, feed from the sources and uses of funds in the transaction

Step II: Build the Pre-LBO Model

Step II(c): Build Cash Flow Statement through Investing Activities

Operating Activities: Income Statement Links

- In building the cash flow statement, all the appropriate income statement items, including net income and non-cash expenses (e.g., D&A, amortization of deferred financing fees), must be linked to the operating activities section of the cash flow statement
- Net income is initially inflated in the pre-LBO model as it excludes the pro forma interest expense and amortization of deferred financing fees associated with the LBO financing structure
- Amortization of deferred financing fees is a non-cash expense that is added back to net income in the post-LBO cash flow statement

($ in millions, fiscal year ending December 31)

Cash Flow Statement

	Year 1 2013	Year 2 2014	Year 3 2015	Year 4 2016	Year 5 2017	Year 6 2018	Year 7 2019	Year 8 2020	Year 9 2021	Year 10 2022
Operating Activities										
Net Income	$345.2	$366.0	$384.3	$399.6	$411.6	$424.0	$436.7	$449.8	$463.3	$477.2
Plus: Depreciation	166.9	176.9	185.8	193.2	199.0	204.9	211.1	217.4	224.0	230.7
Plus: Amortization	55.6	59.0	61.9	64.4	66.3	68.3	70.4	72.5	74.7	76.9
Plus: Amortization of Financing Fees	TO BE LINKED FROM INCOME STATEMENT									

Step II: Build the Pre-LBO Model

Step II(c): Build Cash Flow Statement through Investing Activities (continued)

Operating Activities: Balance Sheet Links

- Each YoY change to a balance sheet account must be accounted for by a corresponding addition or subtraction to the appropriate line item on the cash flow statement
- YoY changes in the target's projected working capital items are calculated in their corresponding line items in the operating activities section of the cash flow statement

($ in millions, fiscal year ending December 31)

Cash Flow Statement

	Projection Period									
	Year 1 2013	Year 2 2014	Year 3 2015	Year 4 2016	Year 5 2017	Year 6 2018	Year 7 2019	Year 8 2020	Year 9 2021	Year 10 2022
Operating Activities										
Net Income	$345.2	$366.0	$384.3	$399.6	$411.6	$424.0	$436.7	$449.8	$463.3	$477.2
Plus: Depreciation	166.9	176.9	185.8	193.2	199.0	204.9	211.1	217.4	224.0	230.7
Plus: Amortization	55.6	59.0	61.9	64.4	66.3	68.3	70.4	72.5	74.7	76.9
Plus: Amortization of Financing Fees	TO BE LINKED FROM INCOME STATEMENT									
Changes in Working Capital Items										
(Inc.) / Dec. in Accounts Receivable	(33.8)	(29.0)	(25.6)	(21.5)	(16.8)	(17.3)	(17.8)	(18.4)	(18.9)	(19.5)
(Inc.) / Dec. in Inventories	(45.0)	(38.7)	(34.2)	(28.7)	(22.4)	(23.1)	(23.8)	(24.5)	(25.2)	(26.0)
(Inc.) / Dec. in Prepaid and Other Current Assets	(13.1)	(11.3)	(10.0)	(8.4)	(6.5)	(6.7)	(6.9)	(7.1)	(7.4)	(7.6)
Inc. / (Dec.) in Accounts Payable	16.1	13.9	12.2	10.3	8.0	8.3	8.5	8.8	9.0	9.3
Inc. / (Dec.) in Accrued Liabilities	20.6	17.7	15.7	13.2	10.3	10.6	10.9	11.2	11.6	11.9
Inc. / (Dec.) in Other Current Liabilities	7.5	6.5	5.7	4.8	3.7	3.8	4.0	4.1	4.2	4.3
(Inc.) / Dec. in Net Working Capital	(47.6)	(41.0)	(36.2)	(30.4)	(23.7)	(24.4)	(25.1)	(25.9)	(26.7)	(27.5)
Cash Flow from Operating Activities	$520.1	$560.9	$595.8	$626.8	$653.2	$672.8	$693.0	$713.8	$735.2	$757.3

Step II: Build the Pre-LBO Model

Step II(c): Build Cash Flow Statement through Investing Activities (continued)

Investing Activities

- Capex is typically the key line item under investing activities, although planned acquisitions or divestitures may also be captured in the other investing activities line item
  - Projected capex assumptions are typically sourced from the CIM and inputted into an assumptions page where they are linked to the cash flow statement
- The target's projected net PP&E must incorporate the capex projections (added to PP&E) as well as those for depreciation (subtracted from PP&E)
- The sum of the annual cash flows provided by operating activities and investing activities provides annual cash flow available for debt repayment, which is commonly referred to as free cash flow

($ in millions, fiscal year ending December 31)

Cash Flow Statement

					Projection Period					
	Year 1 2013	Year 2 2014	Year 3 2015	Year 4 2016	Year 5 2017	Year 6 2018	Year 7 2019	Year 8 2020	Year 9 2021	Year 10 2022
Investing Activitie s										
Capital Expenditures	(166.9)	(176.9)	(185.8)	(193.2)	(199.0)	(204.9)	(211.1)	(217.4)	(224.0)	(230.7)
Other Investing Activities	-	-	-	-	-	-	-	-	-	-
Cash Flow from Investing Activities	($166.9)	($176.9)	($185.8)	($193.2)	($199.0)	($204.9)	($211.1)	($217.4)	($224.0)	($230.7)

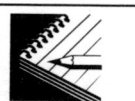

Step II: Build the Pre-LBO Model

Step II(c): Build Cash Flow Statement through Investing Activities (continued)

Financing Activities

- The financing activities section of the cash flow statement is constructed to include line items for the (repayment)/drawdown of each debt instrument in the LBO financing structure
- These line items are initially left blank until the LBO financing structure is entered into the model (Step III) and a detailed debt schedule is built (Step IV(a))

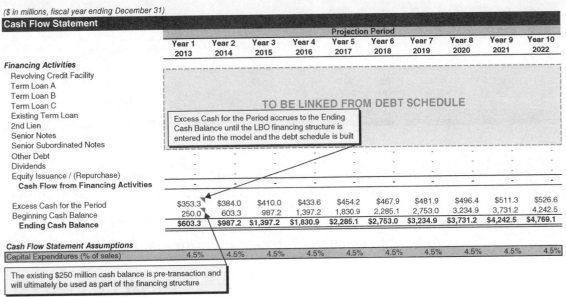

($ in millions, fiscal year ending December 31)

Cash Flow Statement

	Year 1 2013	Year 2 2014	Year 3 2015	Year 4 2016	Year 5 2017	Year 6 2018	Year 7 2019	Year 8 2020	Year 9 2021	Year 10 2022
Financing Activities										
Revolving Credit Facility										
Term Loan A										
Term Loan B										
Term Loan C										
Existing Term Loan										
2nd Lien										
Senior Notes										
Senior Subordinated Notes										
Other Debt	-	-	-	-	-	-	-	-	-	-
Dividends	-	-	-	-	-	-	-	-	-	-
Equity Issuance / (Repurchase)	-	-	-	-	-	-	-	-	-	-
Cash Flow from Financing Activities	-	-	-	-	-	-	-	-	-	-
Excess Cash for the Period	$353.3	$384.0	$410.0	$433.6	$454.2	$467.9	$481.9	$496.4	$511.3	$526.6
Beginning Cash Balance	250.0	603.3	987.2	1,397.2	1,830.9	2,285.1	2,753.0	3,234.9	3,731.2	4,242.5
Ending Cash Balance	$603.3	$987.2	$1,397.2	$1,830.9	$2,285.1	$2,753.0	$3,234.9	$3,731.2	$4,242.5	$4,769.1
Cash Flow Statement Assumptions										
Capital Expenditures (% of sales)	4.5%	4.5%	4.5%	4.5%	4.5%	4.5%	4.5%	4.5%	4.5%	4.5%

TO BE LINKED FROM DEBT SCHEDULE

Excess Cash for the Period accrues to the Ending Cash Balance until the LBO financing structure is entered into the model and the debt schedule is built

The existing $250 million cash balance is pre-transaction and will ultimately be used as part of the financing structure

Step II: Build the Pre-LBO Model

Step II(c): Build Cash Flow Statement through Investing Activities (continued)

Cash Flow Statement Links to Balance Sheet

- Once the cash flow statement is built, ending cash balance for each year in the projection period is linked to the cash and cash equivalents line item in the balance sheet, thereby fully linking the financial statements of the pre-LBO model

($ in millions, fiscal year ending December 31)

Cash Flow Statement

	Projection Period									
	Year 1 2013	Year 2 2014	Year 3 2015	Year 4 2016	Year 5 2017	Year 6 2018	Year 7 2019	Year 8 2020	Year 9 2021	Year 10 2022
Excess Cash for the Period	$353.3	$384.0	$410.0	$433.6	$454.2	$467.9	$481.9	$496.4	$511.3	$526.6
Beginning Cash Balance	250.0	603.3	987.2	1,397.2	1,830.9	2,285.1	2,753.0	3,234.9	3,731.2	4,242.5
Ending Cash Balance	**$603.3**	**$987.2**	**$1,397.2**	**$1,830.9**	**$2,285.1**	**$2,753.0**	**$3,234.9**	**$3,731.2**	**$4,242.5**	**$4,769.1**

Balance Sheet

		Projection Period									
	Pro Forma 2012	Year 1 2013	Year 2 2014	Year 3 2015	Year 4 2016	Year 5 2017	Year 6 2018	Year 7 2019	Year 8 2020	Year 9 2021	Year 10 2022
Cash and Cash Equivalents	$250.0	$603.3	$987.2	$1,397.2	$1,830.9	$2,285.1	$2,753.0	$3,234.9	$3,731.2	$4,242.5	$4,769.1

= Ending Cash Balance₂₀₁₃ₑ
(from Cash Flow Statement)

Step III: Input Transaction Structure

Step III(a): Enter Purchase Price Assumptions

Step III(b): Enter Financing Structure into Sources and Uses

Step III(c): Link Sources and Uses to Balance Sheet Adjustments Columns

Step III: Input Transaction Structure

Step III(a): Enter Purchase Price Assumptions

- A purchase price must be assumed for a given target in order to determine the supporting financing structure (debt and equity)

Purchase Price Assumptions – Private Company

($ in millions)

Purchase Price	
Public / Private Target	**2**
Entry EBITDA Multiple	8.0x
LTM 9/30/2012 EBITDA	700.0
Enterprise Value	**$5,600.0**
Less: Total Debt	(1,500.0)
Less: Preferred Stock	-
Less: Noncontrolling Interest	-
Plus: Cash and Cash Equivalents	250.0
Equity Purchase Price	**$4,350.0**

Enter "1" for a public target
Enter "2" for a private target
*Our LBO model template automatically updates the labels and calculations for each selection (see Exhibit 5.13)

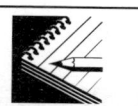

Step III: Input Transaction Structure

Step III(a): Enter Purchase Price Assumptions (continued)

- For a public company, the equity purchase price is calculated by multiplying the offer price per share by the target's fully diluted shares outstanding
- Net debt is then added to the equity purchase price to arrive at an implied enterprise value

Purchase Price Assumptions – Public Company

($ in millions, except per share data)

Purchase Price	
Public / Private Target	1
Offer Price per Share	$54.38
Fully Diluted Shares Outstanding	80.0
Equity Purchase Price	**$4,350.0**
Plus: Total Debt	1,500.0
Plus: Preferred Stock	-
Plus: Noncontrolling Interest	-
Less: Cash and Cash Equivalents	(250.0)
Enterprise Value	**$5,600.0**

Step III: Input Transaction Structure

Step III(b): Enter Financing Structure into Sources and Uses

- A sources and uses table is used to summarize the flow of funds required to consummate a transaction
- Sources of funds refer to the total capital used to finance an acquisition while uses of funds refer to those items funded by the capital sources
- Sum of the sources of funds must equal the sum of the uses of funds

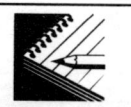

Step III: Input Transaction Structure

($ in millions)

Financing Structures

Sources of Funds	Structure 1	Structure 2	Structure 3	Structure 4	Status Quo
	1	**2**	**3**	**4**	**5**
Revolving Credit Facility Size	$250.0	$250.0	$250.0	$250.0	-
Revolving Credit Facility Draw	-	-	-	-	-
Term Loan A	-	500.0	-	-	-
Term Loan B	2,150.0	1,650.0	2,100.0	1,750.0	-
Term Loan C	-	-	-	-	-
2nd Lien	-	-	-	-	-
Senior Notes	1,500.0	1,500.0	700.0	1,000.0	-
Senior Subordinated Notes	-	-	700.0	1,000.0	-
Equity Contribution	2,100.0	2,100.0	2,250.0	2,250.0	-
Rollover Equity	-	-	-	-	-
Cash on Hand	250.0	250.0	250.0	-	-
	-	-	-	-	-
Total Sources of Funds	**$6,000.0**	**$6,000.0**	**$6,000.0**	**$6,000.0**	**-**
Uses of Funds					
Equity Purchase Price	$4,350.0	$4,350.0	$4,350.0	$4,350.0	-
Repay Existing Bank Debt	1,500.0	1,500.0	1,500.0	1,500.0	-
Tender / Call Premiums	20.0	20.0	20.0	20.0	-
Financing Fees	90.0	90.0	90.0	90.0	-
Other Fees and Expenses	40.0	40.0	40.0	40.0	-
-	-	-	-	-	-
	-	-	-	-	-
Total Uses of Funds	**$6,000.0**	**$6,000.0**	**$6,000.0**	**$6,000.0**	**-**

Step III: Input Transaction Structure

Step III(c): Link Sources and Uses to Balance Sheet Adjustments Columns

- Once the sources and uses of funds are entered into the model, each amount is linked to the appropriate cell in the adjustments columns adjacent to the opening balance sheet
- Any goodwill that is created, however, is calculated on the basis of equity purchase price and net identifiable assets (calculated as shareholders' equity less existing goodwill)
- The equity contribution must also be adjusted to account for any transaction-related fees and expenses (other than financing fees) that are expensed upfront

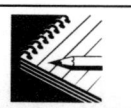

Step IV: Complete the Post-LBO Model

Step IV(a): Build Debt Schedule

Step IV(b): Complete Pro Forma Income Statement from EBIT to Net Income

Step IV(c): Complete Pro Forma Balance Sheet

Step IV(d): Complete Pro Forma Cash Flow Statement

Step IV: Complete the Post-LBO Model

Step IV(a): Build Debt Schedule

- The debt schedule is an integral component of the LBO model, serving to layer in the pro forma effects of the LBO financing structure on the target's financial statements
- Debt schedule enables the banker to:
  - Complete the pro forma income statement from EBIT to net income
  - Complete the pro forma long-term liabilities and shareholders' equity sections of the balance sheet
  - Complete the pro forma financing activities section of the cash flow statement
- Applies free cash flow to make mandatory and optional debt repayments, thereby calculating the annual beginning and ending balances for each debt tranche
  - Debt repayment amounts are linked to the financing activities section of the cash flow statement and the ending debt balances are linked to the balance sheet
- Also used to calculate the annual interest expense for the individual debt instruments, which is linked to the income statement

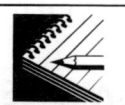

Step IV: Complete the Post-LBO Model

Step IV(a): Build Debt Schedule (continued)

Forward LIBOR Curve

- For floating rate debt instruments, such as revolving credit facilities and term loans, interest rates are typically based on LIBOR plus a fixed spread
- To calculate projected annual interest expense, must first enter future LIBOR estimates for each year of the projection period
- Pricing spreads for the revolver and TLB are added to the forward LIBOR in each year of the projection period to calculate annual interest rates

($ in millions, fiscal year ending December 31)

Debt Schedule

	Pro forma 2012	Year 1 2013	Year 2 2014	Year 3 2015	Year 4 2016	Year 5 2017	Year 6 2018	Year 7 2019	Year 8 2020	Year 9 2021	Year 10 2022
						Projection Period					
Forward LIBOR Curve	0.25%	0.35%	0.50%	0.75%	1.00%	1.25%	1.50%	1.75%	2.00%	2.25%	2.50%

Step IV: Complete the Post-LBO Model

Step IV(a): Build Debt Schedule (continued)

Cash Available for Debt Repayment (Free Cash Flow)

- The annual projected cash available for debt repayment is the sum of the cash flows provided by operating and investing activities on the cash flow statement
  - For each year in the projection period, this amount is first used to make mandatory debt repayments on the term loan tranches
  - Remaining cash flow is used to make optional debt repayments, as calculated in the cash available for optional debt repayment line item
- In addition to internally generated free cash flow, existing cash from the balance sheet may be used ("swept") to make incremental debt repayments
  - In the event the post-LBO balance sheet has a cash balance, it is common to keep a constant minimum level of cash on the balance sheet throughout the projection period by inputting a dollar amount under the "MinCash" heading

Step IV: Complete the Post-LBO Model

Cash Available for Debt Repayment (Free Cash Flow)

($ in millions, fiscal year ending December 31)

Debt Schedule

	Pro forma 2012	Year 1 2013	Year 2 2014	Year 3 2015	Year 4 2016	Year 5 2017	Year 6 2018	Year 7 2019	Year 8 2020	Year 9 2021	Year 10 2022
						Projection Period					
Forward LIBOR Curve	0.25%	0.35%	0.50%	0.75%	1.00%	1.25%	1.50%	1.75%	2.00%	2.25%	2.50%
Cash Flow from Operating Activities		$371.8	$420.5	$464.7	$506.3	$544.5	$575.9	$609.8	$637.1	$657.3	$680.7
Cash Flow from Investing Activities		(166.9)	(176.9)	(185.8)	(193.2)	(199.0)	(204.9)	(211.1)	(217.4)	(224.0)	(230.7)
Cash Available for Debt Repayment		$204.9	$243.6	$278.9	$313.1	$345.5	$371.0	$398.7	$419.7	$433.3	$450.0
Total Mandatory Repayments	MinCash	(21.5)	(21.5)	(21.5)	(21.5)	(21.5)	(21.5)	(21.5)	-	-	-
Cash From Balance Sheet	-	-	-	-	-	-	-	-	5.8	425.4	858.8
Cash Available for Optional Debt Repayment		$183.4	$222.1	$257.4	$291.6	$324.0	$349.5	$377.2	$425.4	$858.8	$1,308.8

= Cash Flow from Operating Activiites$_{2013E}$ + Cash Flow from Investing Activities$_{2013E}$
= $371.8 million + ($166.9) million

= Mandatory Repayments on the Term Loan B, calculated as 1% x $2,150 million

= IF (Cash Balance toggle = 1, then sweep cash from the Balance Sheet less the Minimum Cash Balance, otherwise display 0)

= Cash Flow for Debt Repayment$_{2016E}$ - Total Mandatory Repayments$_{2016E}$
= $313.1 million + ($21.5) million

Step IV: Complete the Post-LBO Model

Step IV(a): Build Debt Schedule (continued)

Revolving Credit Facility

- In the "Revolving Credit Facility" section of the debt schedule, input the spread, term, and commitment fee associated with the facility
- Facility's size is linked from an assumptions page where the financing structure is entered and the beginning balance line item for the first year of the projection period is linked from the balance sheet
- The revolver's drawdown/(repayment) line item feeds from the cash available for optional debt repayment line item at the top of the debt schedule

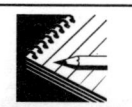

Step IV: Complete the Post-LBO Model

($ in millions, fiscal year ending December 31)

Debt Schedule

	Pro forma 2012		Year 1 2013	Year 2 2014	Year 3 2015	Year 4 2016	Year 5 2017	Year 6 2018	Year 7 2019	Year 8 2020	Year 9 2021	Year 10 2022
						Projection Period						
Forward LIBOR Curve	0.25%		0.35%	0.50%	0.75%	1.00%	1.25%	1.50%	1.75%	2.00%	2.25%	2.50%
Cash Flow from Operating Activities			$371.8	$420.5	$464.7	$506.3	$544.5	$575.9	$609.8	$637.1	$657.3	$680.7
Cash Flow from Investing Activities			(166.9)	(176.9)	(185.8)	(193.2)	(199.0)	(204.9)	(211.1)	(217.4)	(224.0)	(230.7)
Cash Available for Debt Repayment			$204.9	$243.6	$278.9	$313.1	$345.5	$371.0	$398.7	$419.7	$433.3	$450.0
Total Mandatory Repayments	**MinCash**		(21.5)	(21.5)	(21.5)	(21.5)	(21.5)	(21.5)	(21.5)	-	-	-
Cash From Balance Sheet	-		-	-	-	-	-	-	-	5.8	425.4	858.8
Cash Available for Optional Debt Repayment			$183.4	$222.1	$257.4	$291.6	$324.0	$349.5	$377.2	$425.4	$858.8	$1,308.8

Revolving Credit Facility

Revolving Credit Facility Size	$250.0										
Spread	4.250%										
LIBOR Floor	1.250%				= Ending Balance from Prior Year						
Term	6 years										
Commitment Fee on Unused Portion	0.50%			= Ending Revolver Balance from Pro Forma 2012E Balance Sheet							
Beginning Balance			-	-	-	-	-	-	-	-	-
Drawdown/(Repayment)			-	-	-	-	-	-	-	-	-
Ending Balance			-	-	-	-	-	-	-	-	-
Interest Rate		5.50%	5.50%	5.50%	5.50%	5.50%	5.75%	6.00%	6.25%	6.50%	6.75%
Interest Expense		-	-	-	-	-	-	-	-	-	-
Commitment Fee		1.3	1.3	1.3	1.3	1.3	1.3	1.3	1.3	1.3	1.3
Administrative Agent Fee		0.2	0.2	0.2	0.2	0.2	0.2	0.2	0.2	0.2	0.2

= IF (LIBOR floor is greater than LIBOR $_{2013E}$,

then use LIBOR floor, otherwise use LIBOR$_{2013E}$) + Spread

= IF (1.25% > 0.35%, 1.25%, 0.35%) + 4.25%

= Commitment Fee on Unused Portion x (Revolver Capacity - (Average of Beginning Balance$_{2021E}$ and Ending Balance$_{2021E}$))

= 0.50% x $250 million

= IF (Cash Available for Optional Debt Repayment$_{2022E}$ > 0, then sweep the negative value of the minimum of (Cash Available for Optional Debt Repayment$_{2022E}$ vs.

the Beginning Balance$_{2022E}$), otherwise sweep the negative value of the minimum of (Cash Available for Optional Debt Repayment$_{2022E}$ vs. 0))

= IF (Cash Available for Optional Debt Repayment$_{2022E}$ > 0, -MIN(Cash Available for Optional Debt Repayment$_{2022E}$, $0.0), -MIN(Cash Available for Optional Debt Repayment$_{2022E}$, 0))

Step IV: Complete the Post-LBO Model

Step IV(a): Build Debt Schedule (continued)

Term Loan Facility

- In the "Term Loan Facility" section of the debt schedule, the banker inputs the spread, term, and mandatory repayment schedule associated with the facility
- Facility's size is linked from the sources and uses of funds on the transaction summary page

Mandatory Repayments (Amortization)

- Unlike a revolving credit facility, which only requires repayment at the maturity date of all the outstanding advances, a term loan facility is fully funded at close and has a set amortization schedule, typically 1% per year

Optional Repayments

- A typical LBO model employs a "100% cash flow sweep" that assumes all cash generated by the target after making mandatory debt repayments is applied to the optional repayment of outstanding prepayable debt (typically bank debt)
- For modeling purposes, bank debt is generally repaid in the following order: revolver balance, term loan A, term loan B, etc.

Step IV: Complete the Post-LBO Model

($ in millions, fiscal year ending December 31)

Debt Schedule

	Pro forma 2012	Year 1 2013	Year 2 2014	Year 3 2015	Year 4 2016	Year 5 2017	Year 6 2018	Year 7 2019	Year 8 2020	Year 9 2021	Year 10 2022
						Projection Period					
Forward LIBOR Curve	0.25%	0.35%	0.50%	0.75%	1.00%	1.25%	1.50%	1.75%	2.00%	2.25%	2.50%
Cash Flow from Operating Activities		$371.8	$420.5	$464.7	$506.3	$544.5	$575.9	$609.8	$637.1	$657.3	$680.7
Cash Flow from Investing Activities		(166.9)	(176.9)	(185.8)	(193.2)	(199.0)	(204.9)	(211.1)	(217.4)	(224.0)	(230.7)
Cash Available for Debt Repayment		**$204.9**	**$243.6**	**$278.9**	**$313.1**	**$345.5**	**$371.0**	**$398.7**	**$419.7**	**$433.3**	**$450.0**
Total Mandatory Repayments	**MinCash**	(21.5)	(21.5)	(21.5)	(21.5)	(21.5)	(21.5)	(21.5)	-	-	-
Cash From Balance Sheet	-	-	-	-	-	-	-	-	5.8	425.4	858.8
Cash Available for Optional Debt Repayment		**$183.4**	**$222.1**	**$257.4**	**$291.6**	**$324.0**	**$349.5**	**$377.2**	**$425.4**	**$858.8**	**$1,308.8**

Term Loan B Facility

Size	$2,150.0										
Spread	4.500%										
LIBOR Floor	1.250%										
Term	7 years			= Ending Term Loan B Balance from Pro Forma 2012E Balance Sheet							
Repayment Schedule	1.0% Per Annum, Bullet at Maturity										
Beginning Balance		$2,150.0	$1,945.1	$1,701.5	$1,422.6	$1,109.4	$763.9	$392.9	-	-	-
Mandatory Repayments		(21.5)	(21.5)	(21.5)	(21.5)	(21.5)	(21.5)	(21.5)	-	-	-
Optional Repayments		(183.4)	(222.1)	(257.4)	(291.6)	(324.0)	(349.5)	(371.4)	-	-	-
Ending Balance		**$1,945.1**	**$1,701.5**	**$1,422.6**	**$1,109.4**	**$763.9**	**$392.9**	**-**	**-**	**-**	**-**
Interest Rate		5.75%	5.75%	5.75%	5.75%	5.75%	6.00%	6.25%	6.50%	6.75%	7.00%
Interest Expense		117.7	104.8	89.8	72.8	53.9	34.7	12.3	-	-	-

= Interest Rate$_{2013E}$ x Average(Beginning Balance$_{2013E}$:Ending Balance$_{2013E}$)
= 5.75% x Average of $2,150 million and $1,945.1 million

= The negative of the minimum of (Cash Flow Available for Optional Debt Repayment $_{2015E}$
    vs. Beginning Balance$_{2015E}$ + Mandatory Amortization $_{2015E}$)
= -MIN ($257.4 million : $1,701.5 million + ($21.5) million)

= IF (Beginning Balance$_{2018E}$ is greater than 0 and greater than 1% of the principal amount,
    then subtract 1% Mandatory Amortization on the principal amount of the Term Loan B, otherwise display $0.0)
= IF ($763.9 million > 0 and > 1% x $2,150 million, then 1% x $2,150 million, otherwise $0.0)

Step IV: Complete the Post-LBO Model

($ in millions, fiscal year ending December 31)

Debt Schedule

	Pro forma 2012	Year 1 2013	Year 2 2014	Year 3 2015	Year 4 2016	Year 5 2017	Year 6 2018	Year 7 2019	Year 8 2020	Year 9 2021	Year 10 2022
						Projection Period					
Forward LIBOR Curve	0.25%	0.35%	0.50%	0.75%	1.00%	1.25%	1.50%	1.75%	2.00%	2.25%	2.50%
Cash Flow from Operating Activities		$371.8	$420.5	$464.7	$506.3	$544.5	$575.9	$609.8	$637.1	$657.3	$680.7
Cash Flow from Investing Activities		(166.9)	(176.9)	(185.8)	(193.2)	(199.0)	(204.9)	(211.1)	(217.4)	(224.0)	(230.7)
Cash Available for Debt Repayment		$204.9	$243.6	$278.9	$313.1	$345.5	$371.0	$398.7	$419.7	$433.3	$450.0
Total Mandatory Repayments	MinCash	(21.5)	(21.5)	(21.5)	(21.5)	(21.5)	(21.5)	(21.5)	-	-	-
Cash From Balance Sheet	-	-	-	-	-	-	-	-	5.8	425.4	858.8
Cash Available for Optional Debt Repayment		$183.4	$222.1	$257.4	$291.6	$324.0	$349.5	$377.2	$425.4	$858.8	$1,308.8

Revolving Credit Facility

Revolving Credit Facility Size	$250.0										
Spread	4.250%										
LIBOR Floor	1.250%										
Term	6 years										
Commitment Fee on Unused Portion	0.50%										
Beginning Balance		-	-	-	-	-	-	-	-	-	-
Drawdown/(Repayment)		-	-	-	-	-	-	-	-	-	-
Ending Balance		-	-	-	-	-	-	-	-	-	-
Interest Rate		5.50%	5.50%	5.50%	5.50%	5.50%	5.75%	6.00%	6.25%	6.50%	6.75%
Interest Expense		-	-	-	-	-	-	-	-	-	-
Commitment Fee		1.3	1.3	1.3	1.3	1.3	1.3	1.3	1.3	1.3	1.3
Administrative Agent Fee		0.2	0.2	0.2	0.2	0.2	0.2	0.2	0.2	0.2	0.2

Term Loan B Facility

Size	$2,150.0										
Spread	4.500%										
LIBOR Floor	1.250%										
Term	7 years										
Repayment Schedule	1.0%	Per Annum, Bullet at Maturity									
Beginning Balance		$2,150.0	$1,945.1	$1,701.5	$1,422.6	$1,109.4	$763.9	$392.9	-	-	-
Mandatory Repayments		(21.5)	(21.5)	(21.5)	(21.5)	(21.5)	(21.5)	(21.5)	-	-	-
Optional Repayments		(183.4)	(222.1)	(257.4)	(291.6)	(324.0)	(349.5)	(371.4)	-	-	-
Ending Balance		$1,945.1	$1,701.5	$1,422.6	$1,109.4	$763.9	$392.9	-	-	-	-
Interest Rate		5.75%	5.75%	5.75%	5.75%	5.75%	6.00%	6.25%	6.50%	6.75%	7.00%
Interest Expense		117.7	104.8	89.8	72.8	53.9	34.7	12.3	-	-	-

Senior Notes

Size	$1,500.0										
Coupon	8.500%										
Term	8 years										
Beginning Balance		$1,500.0	$1,500.0	$1,500.0	$1,500.0	$1,500.0	$1,500.0	$1,500.0	$1,500.0	$1,500.0	$1,500.0
Repayment		-	-	-	-	-	-	-	-	-	-
Ending Balance		$1,500.0	$1,500.0	$1,500.0	$1,500.0	$1,500.0	$1,500.0	$1,500.0	$1,500.0	$1,500.0	$1,500.0
Interest Expense		127.5	127.5	127.5	127.5	127.5	127.5	127.5	127.5	127.5	127.5

Step IV: Complete the Post-LBO Model

Step IV(b): Complete Pro Forma Income Statement from EBIT to Net Income

- The calculated average annual interest expense for each loan, bond, or other debt instrument in the capital structure is linked from the completed debt schedule to its corresponding line item on the income statement

Cash Interest Expense

- Refers to a company's actual cash interest and associated financing-related payments in a given year
- It is the sum of the average interest expense for each cash-pay debt instrument plus the commitment fee on the unused portion of the revolver and the administrative agent fee

Total Interest Expense

- Sum of cash and non-cash interest expense, most notably the amortization of deferred financing fees, which is linked from an assumptions page

Net Income

- Subtract net interest expense from EBIT, which creates earnings before taxes (EBT)
- Multiply EBT by target's marginal tax rate to produce tax expense, which is netted out of EBT to calculate net income
- Net income for each year in the projection period is linked from the income statement to the cash flow statement as the first line item under operating activities

---

Step IV: Complete the Post-LBO Model

($ in millions, fiscal year ending December 31)

Income Statement

	Pro forma 2012	Year 1 2013	Year 2 2014	Year 3 2015	Year 4 2016	Year 5 2017	Year 6 2018	Year 7 2019	Year 8 2020	Year 9 2021	Year 10 2022
						Projection Period					
EBIT	$518.0	$556.9	$590.3	$619.8	$644.6	$663.9	$683.8	$704.3	$725.5	$747.2	$769.6
% margin	15.0%	15.0%	15.0%	15.0%	15.0%	15.0%	15.0%	15.0%	15.0%	15.0%	15.0%
Interest Expense	-	-	-	-	-	-	-	-	-	-	-
Revolving Credit Facility	-	-	-	-	-	-	-	-	-	-	-
Term Loan A	-	-	-	-	-	-	-	-	-	-	-
Term Loan B	123.6	117.7	104.8	89.8	72.8	53.9	34.7	12.3	-	-	-
Term Loan C	-	-	-	-	-	-	-	-	-	-	-
Existing Term Loan	-	-	-	-	-	-	-	-	-	-	-
2nd Lien	-	-	-	-	-	-	-	-	-	-	-
Senior Notes	127.5	127.5	127.5	127.5	127.5	127.5	127.5	127.5	127.5	127.5	127.5
Senior Subordinated Notes	-	-	-	-	-	-	-	-	-	-	-
Commitment Fee on Unused Revolver	1.3	1.3	1.3	1.3	1.3	1.3	1.3	1.3	1.3	1.3	1.3
Administrative Agent Fee	0.2	0.2	0.2	0.2	0.2	0.2	0.2	0.2	0.2	0.2	0.2
Cash Interest Expense	$252.5	$246.6	$233.7	$218.7	$201.7	$182.8	$163.6	$141.2	$128.9	$128.9	$128.9
Amortization of Deferred Financing Fees	12.0	12.0	12.0	12.0	12.0	12.0	12.0	11.4	6.8	-	-
Total Interest Expense	$264.5	$258.6	$245.7	$230.7	$213.7	$194.7	$175.6	$152.5	$135.7	$128.9	$128.9
Interest Income		-	-	-	-	-	-	(0.0)	(1.1)	(3.2)	(5.4)
Net Interest Expense		$258.6	$245.7	$230.7	$213.7	$194.7	$175.6	$152.5	$134.6	$125.7	$123.5
Earnings Before Taxes		298.2	344.5	389.1	430.9	469.2	508.2	551.8	590.9	621.5	646.2
Income Tax Expense		113.3	130.9	147.8	163.7	178.3	193.1	209.7	224.5	236.2	245.5
Net Income		$184.9	$213.6	$241.2	$267.2	$290.9	$315.1	$342.1	$366.4	$385.4	$400.6
% margin		5.0%	5.4%	5.8%	6.2%	6.6%	6.9%	7.3%	7.6%	7.7%	7.8%

Step IV: Complete the Post-LBO Model

Step IV(c): Complete Pro Forma Balance Sheet

Liabilities

- The balance sheet is completed by linking the year-end balances for each debt instrument directly from the debt schedule
- The remaining non-current and non-debt liabilities, captured in the other long-term liabilities line item, are generally held constant at the prior year level in the absence of specific management guidance

Shareholders' Equity

- Pro forma net income, which has now been calculated for each year in the projection period, is added to the prior year's shareholders' equity as retained earnings

Step IV(d): Complete Pro Forma Cash Flow Statement

- To complete the cash flow statement, the mandatory and optional repayments for each debt instrument, as calculated in the debt schedule, are linked to the appropriate line items in the financing activities section and summed to produce the annual repayment amounts
- Annual pro forma beginning and ending cash balances are then calculated accordingly

Step IV: Complete the Post-LBO Model

($ in millions, fiscal year ending December 31)

Balance Sheet

	Opening 2012	Adjustments +	Adjustments −	Pro Forma 2012	Year 1 2013	Year 2 2014	Year 3 2015	Year 4 2016	Year 5 2017	Year 6 2018	Year 7 2019	Year 8 2020	Year 9 2021	Year 10 2022
									Projection Period					
Cash and Cash Equivalents	$250.0		(250.0)	-	-	-	-	-	-	-	$5.8	$425.4	$858.8	$1,308.8
Accounts Receivable	450.0			450.0	483.8	512.8	538.4	560.0	576.7	594.1	611.9	630.2	649.1	668.6
Inventories	600.0			600.0	645.0	683.7	717.9	746.6	769.0	792.1	815.8	840.3	865.5	891.5
Prepaids and Other Current Assets	175.0			175.0	188.1	199.4	209.4	217.8	224.3	231.0	238.0	245.1	252.4	260.0
Total Current Assets	**$1,475.0**			**$1,225.0**	**$1,316.9**	**$1,395.9**	**$1,465.7**	**$1,524.3**	**$1,570.0**	**$1,617.1**	**$1,671.4**	**$2,141.1**	**$2,625.8**	**$3,128.9**
Property, Plant and Equipment, net	2,500.0			2,500.0	2,500.0	2,500.0	2,500.0	2,500.0	2,500.0	2,500.0	2,500.0	2,500.0	2,500.0	2,500.0
Goodwill	1,000.0	1,850.0	(1,000.0)	1,850.0	1,850.0	1,850.0	1,850.0	1,850.0	1,850.0	1,850.0	1,850.0	1,850.0	1,850.0	1,850.0
Intangible Assets	875.0			875.0	819.4	760.4	698.5	634.1	567.8	499.4	429.1	356.8	282.0	205.1
Other Assets	150.0			150.0	150.0	150.0	150.0	150.0	150.0	150.0	150.0	150.0	150.0	150.0
Deferred Financing Fees	-	90.0		90.0	78.0	66.0	54.1	42.1	30.1	18.1	6.7	-	-	-
Total Assets	**$6,000.0**			**$6,690.0**	**$6,714.3**	**$6,722.3**	**$6,718.2**	**$6,700.5**	**$6,667.9**	**$6,634.7**	**$6,607.2**	**$6,997.7**	**$7,407.8**	**$7,834.0**
Accounts Payable	215.0			215.0	231.1	245.0	257.2	267.5	275.6	283.8	292.3	301.1	310.1	319.4
Accrued Liabilities	275.0			275.0	295.8	313.4	329.0	342.2	352.5	363.0	373.9	385.1	396.7	408.6
Other Current Liabilities	100.0			100.0	107.5	114.0	119.6	124.4	128.2	132.0	136.0	140.1	144.3	148.6
Total Current Liabilities	**$590.0**			**$590.0**	**$634.3**	**$672.3**	**$705.9**	**$734.2**	**$756.2**	**$778.9**	**$802.2**	**$826.3**	**$851.1**	**$876.6**
Revolving Credit Facility	-			-	-	-	-	-	-	-	-	-	-	-
Term Loan A	-			-										
Term Loan B	-	2,150.0		2,150.0	1,945.1	1,701.5	1,422.6	1,109.4	763.9	392.9	-	-	-	-
Term Loan C	-			-										
Existing Term Loan	1,000.0		(1,000.0)	-	-	-	-	-	-	-	-	-	-	-
2nd Lien	-			-										
Senior Notes	-	1,500.0		1,500.0	1,500.0	1,500.0	1,500.0	1,500.0	1,500.0	1,500.0	1,500.0	1,500.0	1,500.0	1,500.0
Existing Senior Notes	500.0		(500.0)	-	-	-	-	-	-	-	-	-	-	-
Senior Subordinated Notes	-			-										
Other Debt	-			-										
Deferred Income Taxes	300.0			300.0	300.0	300.0	300.0	300.0	300.0	300.0	300.0	300.0	300.0	300.0
Other Long-Term Liabilities	110.0			110.0	110.0	110.0	110.0	110.0	110.0	110.0	110.0	110.0	110.0	110.0
Total Liabilities	**$2,500.0**			**$4,650.0**	**$4,489.4**	**$4,283.8**	**$4,038.5**	**$3,753.6**	**$3,430.1**	**$3,081.8**	**$2,712.2**	**$2,736.3**	**$2,761.1**	**$2,786.6**
Noncontrolling Interest	-			-										
Shareholders' Equity	3,500.0	2,040.0	(3,500.0)	2,040.0	2,224.9	2,438.5	2,679.7	2,946.9	3,237.8	3,552.9	3,895.0	4,261.4	4,646.7	5,047.3
Total Shareholders' Equity	**$3,500.0**			**$2,040.0**	**$2,224.9**	**$2,438.5**	**$2,679.7**	**$2,946.9**	**$3,237.8**	**$3,552.9**	**$3,895.0**	**$4,261.4**	**$4,646.7**	**$5,047.3**
Total Liabilities and Equity	**$6,000.0**			**$6,690.0**	**$6,714.3**	**$6,722.3**	**$6,718.2**	**$6,700.5**	**$6,667.9**	**$6,634.7**	**$6,607.2**	**$6,997.7**	**$7,407.8**	**$7,834.0**
Balance Check	0.000			0.000	0.000	0.000	0.000	0.000	0.000	0.000	0.000	0.000	0.000	0.000
Net Working Capital	635.0			635.0	682.6	723.6	759.8	790.2	813.9	838.3	863.4	889.3	916.0	943.5
(Increase) / Decrease in Net Working Capital				-	(47.6)	(41.0)	(36.2)	(30.4)	(23.7)	(24.4)	(25.1)	(25.9)	(26.7)	(27.5)

Balance Sheet Assumptions

Current Assets

Days Sales Outstanding (DSO)	47.6			47.6	47.6	47.6	47.6	47.6	47.6	47.6	47.6	47.6	47.6	47.6
Days Inventory Held (DIH)	105.8			105.8	105.8	105.8	105.8	105.8	105.8	105.8	105.8	105.8	105.8	105.8
Prepaid and Other Current Assets (% of sales)	5.1%			5.1%	5.1%	5.1%	5.1%	5.1%	5.1%	5.1%	5.1%	5.1%	5.1%	5.1%

Current Liabilities

Days Payable Outstanding (DPO)	37.9			37.9	37.9	37.9	37.9	37.9	37.9	37.9	37.9	37.9	37.9	37.9
Accrued Liabilities (% of sales)	8.0%			8.0%	8.0%	8.0%	8.0%	8.0%	8.0%	8.0%	8.0%	8.0%	8.0%	8.0%
Other Current Liabilities (% of sales)	2.9%			2.9%	2.9%	2.9%	2.9%	2.9%	2.9%	2.9%	2.9%	2.9%	2.9%	2.9%

Step IV: Complete the Post-LBO Model

($ in millions, fiscal year ending December 31)

Cash Flow Statement

	Year 1 2013	Year 2 2014	Year 3 2015	Year 4 2016	Year 5 2017	Year 6 2018	Year 7 2019	Year 8 2020	Year 9 2021	Year 10 2022
Operating Activities										
Net Income	$184.9	$213.6	$241.2	$267.2	$290.9	$315.1	$342.1	$366.4	$385.4	$400.6
Plus: Depreciation	166.9	176.9	185.8	193.2	199.0	204.9	211.1	217.4	224.0	230.7
Plus: Amortization	55.6	59.0	61.9	64.4	66.3	68.3	70.4	72.5	74.7	76.9
Plus: Amortization of Financing Fees	12.0	12.0	12.0	12.0	12.0	12.0	11.4	6.8	-	-
Changes in Working Capital Items										
(Inc.) / Dec. in Accounts Receivable	(33.8)	(29.0)	(25.6)	(21.5)	(16.8)	(17.3)	(17.8)	(18.4)	(18.9)	(19.5)
(Inc.) / Dec. in Inventories	(45.0)	(38.7)	(34.2)	(28.7)	(22.4)	(23.1)	(23.8)	(24.5)	(25.2)	(26.0)
(Inc.) / Dec. in Prepaid and Other Current Assets	(13.1)	(11.3)	(10.0)	(8.4)	(6.5)	(6.7)	(6.9)	(7.1)	(7.4)	(7.6)
Inc. / (Dec.) in Accounts Payable	16.1	13.9	12.2	10.3	8.0	8.3	8.5	8.8	9.0	9.3
Inc. / (Dec.) in Accrued Liabilities	20.6	17.7	15.7	13.2	10.3	10.6	10.9	11.2	11.6	11.9
Inc. / (Dec.) in Other Current Liabilities	7.5	6.5	5.7	4.8	3.7	3.8	4.0	4.1	4.2	4.3
(Inc.) / Dec. in Net Working Capital	(47.6)	(41.0)	(36.2)	(30.4)	(23.7)	(24.4)	(25.1)	(25.9)	(26.7)	(27.5)
Cash Flow from Operating Activities	**$371.8**	**$420.5**	**$464.7**	**$506.3**	**$544.5**	**$575.9**	**$609.8**	**$637.1**	**$657.3**	**$680.7**
Investing Activities										
Capital Expenditures	(166.9)	(176.9)	(185.8)	(193.2)	(199.0)	(204.9)	(211.1)	(217.4)	(224.0)	(230.7)
Other Investing Activities	-	-	-	-	-	-	-	-	-	-
Cash Flow from Investing Activities	**($166.9)**	**($176.9)**	**($185.8)**	**($193.2)**	**($199.0)**	**($204.9)**	**($211.1)**	**($217.4)**	**($224.0)**	**($230.7)**
Financing Activities										
Revolving Credit Facility	-	-	-	-	-	-	-	-	-	-
Term Loan B	(204.9)	(243.6)	(278.9)	(313.1)	(345.5)	(371.0)	(392.9)	-	-	-
Existing Term Loan	-	-	-	-	-	-	-	-	-	-
Senior Notes	-	-	-	-	-	-	-	-	-	-
Dividends	-	-	-	-	-	-	-	-	-	-
Equity Issuance / (Repurchase)	-	-	-	-	-	-	-	-	-	-
Cash Flow from Financing Activities	**($204.9)**	**($243.6)**	**($278.9)**	**($313.1)**	**($345.5)**	**($371.0)**	**($392.9)**	**-**	**-**	**-**
Excess Cash for the Period	-	-	-	-	-	-	$5.8	$419.7	$433.3	$450.0
Beginning Cash Balance	-	-	-	-	-	-	-	5.8	425.4	858.8
Ending Cash Balance	**-**	**-**	**-**	**-**	**-**	**-**	**$5.8**	**$425.4**	**$858.8**	**$1,308.8**

Cash Flow Statement Assumptions

Capital Expenditures (% of sales)	4.5%	4.5%	4.5%	4.5%	4.5%	4.5%	4.5%	4.5%	4.5%	4.5%

Step V: Perform LBO Analysis

Step V(a): Analyze Financing Structure

Step V(b): Perform Returns Analysis

Step V(c): Determine Valuation

Step V(d): Create Transaction Summary Page

Step V: Perform LBO Analysis

Step V(a): Analyze Financing Structure

- A central part of LBO analysis is the crafting of an optimal financing structure for a given transaction
- From an underwriting perspective, this involves determining whether the target's financial projections can support a given leveraged financing structure under various business and economic conditions
- A key credit risk management concern for the underwriters centers on the target's ability to service its annual interest expense and repay all (or a substantial portion) of its bank debt within the proposed tenor
- The primary credit metrics used to analyze the target's ability to support a given capital structure include variations of the leverage and coverage ratios outlined in Chapter 1 (e.g., debt-to-EBITDA, debt-to-total capitalization, and EBITDA-to-interest expense)
- The next slide displays a typical output summarizing the target's key financial data as well as pro forma capitalization and credit statistics for each year in the projection period

Step V: Perform LBO Analysis

($ in millions, fiscal year ending December 31)

Summary Financial Data

	LTM 9/30/2012	Pro forma 2012	Year 1 2013	Year 2 2014	Year 3 2015	Year 4 2016	Year 5 2017	Year 6 2018	Year 7 2019	Year 8 2020	Year 9 2021	Year 10 2022
						Projection Period						
Sales	$3,385.0	$3,450.0	$3,708.8	$3,931.3	$4,127.8	$4,293.0	$4,421.7	$4,554.4	$4,691.0	$4,831.8	$4,976.7	$5,126.0
% growth	NA	7.8%	7.5%	6.0%	5.0%	4.0%	3.0%	3.0%	3.0%	3.0%	3.0%	3.0%
Gross Profit	$1,350.0	$1,380.0	$1,483.5	$1,572.5	$1,651.1	$1,717.2	$1,768.7	$1,821.8	$1,876.4	$1,932.7	$1,990.7	$2,050.4
% margin	39.9%	40.0%	40.0%	40.0%	40.0%	40.0%	40.0%	40.0%	40.0%	40.0%	40.0%	40.0%
EBITDA	$700.0	$725.0	$779.4	$826.1	$867.4	$902.1	$929.2	$957.1	$985.8	$1,015.4	$1,045.8	$1,077.2
% margin	20.7%	21.0%	21.0%	21.0%	21.0%	21.0%	21.0%	21.0%	21.0%	21.0%	21.0%	21.0%
Capital Expenditures	152.3	155.3	166.9	176.9	185.8	193.2	199.0	204.9	211.1	217.4	224.0	230.7
% sales	4.5%	4.5%	4.5%	4.5%	4.5%	4.5%	4.5%	4.5%	4.5%	4.5%	4.5%	4.5%
Cash Interest Expense	-	252.5	246.6	233.7	218.7	201.7	182.8	163.6	141.2	128.9	128.9	128.9
Total Interest Expense	-	264.5	258.6	245.7	230.7	213.7	194.7	175.6	152.5	135.7	128.9	128.9
Free Cash Flow												
EBITDA			$779.4	$826.1	$867.4	$902.1	$929.2	$957.1	$985.8	$1,015.4	$1,045.8	$1,077.2
Less: Cash Interest Expense			(246.6)	(233.7)	(218.7)	(201.7)	(182.8)	(163.6)	(141.2)	(128.9)	(128.9)	(128.9)
Plus: Interest Income			-	-	-	-	-	-	0.0	1.1	3.2	5.4
Less: Income Taxes			(113.3)	(130.9)	(147.8)	(163.7)	(178.3)	(193.1)	(209.7)	(224.5)	(236.2)	(245.5)
Less: Capital Expenditures			(166.9)	(176.9)	(185.8)	(193.2)	(199.0)	(204.9)	(211.1)	(217.4)	(224.0)	(230.7)
Less: Increase in Net Working Capital			(47.8)	(41.0)	(36.2)	(30.4)	(23.7)	(24.4)	(26.1)	(25.9)	(26.7)	(27.5)
Free Cash Flow			$204.9	$243.6	$278.9	$313.1	$345.5	$371.0	$398.7	$419.7	$433.3	$450.0
Cumulative Free Cash Flow			204.9	448.5	727.4	1,040.6	1,386.1	1,757.1	2,155.8	2,575.4	3,008.8	3,458.8

Capitalization

			Year 1	Year 2	Year 3	Year 4	Year 5	Year 6	Year 7	Year 8	Year 9	Year 10
Cash	-	-	-	-	-	-	-	-	$5.8	$425.4	$858.8	$1,308.8
Revolving Credit Facility		-	-	-	-	-	-	-	-	-	-	-
Term Loan A		-	-	-	-	-	-	-	-	-	-	-
Term Loan B		2,150.0	1,945.1	1,701.5	1,422.6	1,109.4	763.9	392.9	-	-	-	-
Term Loan C		-	-	-	-	-	-	-	-	-	-	-
Existing Term Loan		-	-	-	-	-	-	-	-	-	-	-
2nd Lien		-	-	-	-	-	-	-	-	-	-	-
Other Debt		-	-	-	-	-	-	-	-	-	-	-
Total Senior Secured Debt		$2,150.0	$1,945.1	$1,701.5	$1,422.6	$1,109.4	$763.9	$392.9	-	-	-	-
Senior Notes		1,500.0	1,500.0	1,500.0	1,500.0	1,500.0	1,500.0	1,500.0	1,500.0	1,500.0	1,500.0	1,500.0
Total Senior Debt		$3,650.0	$3,445.1	$3,201.5	$2,922.6	$2,609.4	$2,263.9	$1,892.9	$1,500.0	$1,500.0	$1,500.0	$1,500.0
Senior Subordinated Notes		-	-	-	-	-	-	-	-	-	-	-
Total Debt		$3,650.0	$3,445.1	$3,201.5	$2,922.6	$2,609.4	$2,263.9	$1,892.9	$1,500.0	$1,500.0	$1,500.0	$1,500.0
Shareholders' Equity		2,040.0	2,224.9	2,438.5	2,679.7	2,946.9	3,237.8	3,552.9	3,895.0	4,261.4	4,646.7	5,047.3
Total Capitalization		$5,690.0	$5,670.0	$5,640.0	$5,602.3	$5,556.3	$5,501.7	$5,445.8	$5,395.0	$5,761.4	$6,146.7	$6,547.3
% of Bank Debt Repaid		-	9.5%	20.9%	33.8%	48.4%	64.5%	81.7%	100.0%	100.0%	100.0%	100.0%

> In Year 7, 100% of ValueCo's bank debt is repaid

Credit Statistics

		Year 1	Year 2	Year 3	Year 4	Year 5	Year 6	Year 7	Year 8	Year 9	Year 10
% Debt / Total Capitalization	64.1%	60.8%	56.8%	52.2%	47.0%	41.1%	34.8%	27.8%	26.0%	24.4%	22.9%
EBITDA / Cash Interest Expense	2.9x	3.2x	3.5x	4.0x	4.5x	5.1x	5.8x	7.0x	7.9x	8.1x	8.4x
(EBITDA - Capex) / Cash Interest Expense	2.3x	2.5x	2.8x	3.1x	3.5x	4.0x	4.6x	5.5x	6.2x	6.4x	6.6x
EBITDA / Total Interest Expense	2.7x	3.0x	3.4x	3.8x	4.2x	4.8x	5.5x	6.5x	7.5x	8.1x	8.4x
(EBITDA - Capex) / Total Interest Expense	2.2x	2.4x	2.6x	3.0x	3.3x	3.7x	4.3x	5.1x	5.9x	6.4x	6.6x
Senior Secured Debt / EBITDA	3.0x	2.5x	2.1x	1.6x	1.2x	0.8x	0.4x	- x	- x	- x	- x
Senior Debt / EBITDA	5.0x	4.4x	3.9x	3.4x	2.9x	2.4x	2.0x	1.5x	1.5x	1.4x	1.4x
Total Debt / EBITDA	5.0x	4.4x	3.9x	3.4x	2.9x	2.4x	2.0x	1.5x	1.5x	1.4x	1.4x
Net Debt / EBITDA	5.0x	4.4x	3.9x	3.4x	2.9x	2.4x	2.0x	1.5x	1.1x	0.6x	0.2x

Step V: Perform LBO Analysis

Step V(b): Perform Returns Analysis

- After analyzing the contemplated financing structure from a debt repayment and credit statistics perspective, determine whether it provides sufficient returns to the sponsor given the proposed purchase price and equity contribution
- Sponsors have historically sought 20%+ IRRs in assessing acquisition opportunities
- If the implied returns are too low, both the purchase price and financing structure need to be revisited
- IRRs are driven primarily by the target's projected financial performance, the assumed purchase price and financing structure (particularly the size of the equity contribution), and the assumed exit multiple and year (assuming a sale)
- Although a sponsor may realize a monetization or exit through various strategies and timeframes, a traditional LBO analysis contemplates a full exit via a sale of the entire company in five years

Step V: Perform LBO Analysis

Step V(b): Perform Returns Analysis (continued)

Return Assumptions

- In a traditional LBO analysis, it is common practice to conservatively assume an exit multiple equal to (or below) the entry multiple

Calculation of Enterprise Value and Equity Value at Exit

($ in millions)

Calculation of Exit Enterprise Value and Equity Value (assumes 8.0x exit multiple and 2017E exit year)	Year 5 2017
2017E EBITDA	$929.2
Exit EBITDA Multiple	8.0x
Enterprise Value at Exit	**$7,433.7**
Less: Net Debt	
Revolving Credit Facility	-
Term Loan B	763.9
Senior Notes	1,500.0
Total Debt	**$2,263.9**
Less: Cash and Cash Equivalents	-
Net Debt	**$2,263.9**
Equity Value at Exit	**$5,169.7**

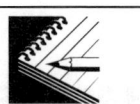

Step V: Perform LBO Analysis

Step V(b): Perform Returns Analysis (continued)

IRR and Cash Return Calculations

- Assuming no additional cash inflows (dividends to the sponsor) or outflows (additional investment by the sponsor) during the investment period, IRR and cash return are calculated on the basis of the sponsor's initial equity contribution (outflow) and the assumed equity proceeds at exit (inflow)
- The initial equity contribution represents a cash outflow for the sponsor
- Cash distributions to the sponsor, such as proceeds received at exit or dividends received during the investment period, are shown as positive values on the timeline

($ in millions)

	Pro forma 2012	Year 1 2013	Year 2 2014	Year 3 2015	Year 4 2016	Year 5 2017
Initial Equity Investment	($2,100.0)					
Dividends / (Investment)	-	-	-	-	-	-
Equity Value at Exit	-	-	-	-	-	5,169.7
Total	**($2,100.0)**	**-**	**-**	**-**	**-**	**$5,169.7**
IRR	20%					
Cash Return	2.5x					

= IRR (Initial Equity Investment : Equity Value at Exit)
= IRR (-$2,100 million : $5,169.7 million)

= Equity Value at Exit / Initial Equity Investment
= $5,169.7 million / $2,100 million

Step V: Perform LBO Analysis

Step V(b): Perform Returns Analysis (continued)

Returns at Various Exit Years

- On the next slide, we calculated IRR and cash return assuming an exit at the end of each year in the projection period using a fixed 8.0x EBITDA exit multiple
- As we progress through the projection period, equity value increases due to the increasing EBITDA and decreasing net debt
- Cash return increases as it is a function of the fixed initial equity investment and increasing equity value at exit

Step V: Perform LBO Analysis

($ in millions, fiscal year ending December 31)

Returns Analysis

		Pro forma 2012				Projection Period						
			Year 1 2013	Year 2 2014	Year 3 2015	Year 4 2016	Year 5 2017	Year 6 2018	Year 7 2019	Year 8 2020	Year 9 2021	Year 10 2022
Entry EBITDA Multiple	8.0x											
Initial Equity Investment		$2,100.0										
EBITDA			$779.4	$826.1	$867.4	$902.1	$929.2	$957.1	$985.8	$1,015.4	$1,045.8	$1,077.2
Exit EBITDA Multiple	8.0x											
Enterprise Value at Exit			$6,235.0	$6,609.1	$6,939.6	$7,217.1	$7,433.7	$7,656.7	$7,886.4	$8,123.0	$8,366.6	$8,617.6
Less: Net Debt												
Revolving Credit Facility			-	-	-	-	-	-	-	-	-	-
Term Loan A			-	-	-	-	-	-	-	-	-	-
Term Loan B			1,945.1	1,701.5	1,422.6	1,109.4	763.9	392.9	-	-	-	-
Term Loan C			-	-	-	-	-	-	-	-	-	-
Existing Term Loan			-	-	-	-	-	-	-	-	-	-
2nd Lien			-	-	-	-	-	-	-	-	-	-
Senior Notes			1,500.0	1,500.0	1,500.0	1,500.0	1,500.0	1,500.0	1,500.0	1,500.0	1,500.0	1,500.0
Senior Subordinated Notes			-	-	-	-	-	-	-	-	-	-
Other Debt			-	-	-	-	-	-	-	-	-	-
Total Debt			$3,445.1	$3,201.5	$2,922.6	$2,609.4	$2,263.9	$1,892.9	$1,500.0	$1,500.0	$1,500.0	$1,500.0
Less: Cash and Cash Equivalents			-	-	-	-	-	-	5.8	425.4	858.8	1,308.8
Net Debt			$3,445.1	$3,201.5	$2,922.6	$2,609.4	$2,263.9	$1,892.9	$1,494.2	$1,074.6	$641.2	$191.2
Equity Value at Exit			$2,789.9	$3,407.6	$4,017.0	$4,607.7	$5,169.7	$5,763.7	$6,392.1	$7,048.4	$7,725.4	$8,426.4

Cash Return	1.3x	1.6x	1.9x	2.2x	2.5x	2.7x	3.0x	3.4x	3.7x	4.0x

	Year 1 2013	Year 2 2014	Year 3 2015	Year 4 2016	Year 5 2017	Year 6 2018	Year 7 2019	Year 8 2020	Year 9 2021	Year 10 2022
Initial Equity Investment	($2,100.0)	($2,100.0)	($2,100.0)	($2,100.0)	($2,100.0)	($2,100.0)	($2,100.0)	($2,100.0)	($2,100.0)	($2,100.0)
Equity Proceeds	$2,789.9									
		$3,407.6								
			$4,017.0							
				$4,607.7						
					$5,169.7					
						$5,763.7				
							$6,392.1			
								$7,048.4		
									$7,725.4	
										$8,426.4

IRR	32.9%	27.4%	24.1%	21.7%	19.7%	18.3%	17.2%	16.3%	15.6%	14.9%

Step V: Perform LBO Analysis

Step V(b): Perform Returns Analysis (continued)

IRR Sensitivity Analysis

- Sensitivity analysis is critical for analyzing IRRs and framing LBO valuation
- IRR can be sensitized for several key value drivers, such as entry and exit multiple, exit year, leverage level, and equity contribution percentage, as well as key operating assumptions such as growth rates and margins
- It is also common to perform sensitivity analysis on a combination of exit multiples and exit years

IRR - Assuming Exit in 2017E

		Exit Multiple				
		7.0x	7.5x	8.0x	8.5x	9.0x
Entry Multiple	7.0x	24.8%	27.4%	29.9%	32.1%	34.2%
	7.5x	19.4%	21.9%	24.2%	26.3%	28.4%
	8.0x	15.1%	17.5%	19.7%	21.8%	23.8%
	8.5x	11.6%	13.9%	16.1%	18.1%	20.0%
	9.0x	8.6%	10.9%	13.0%	15.0%	16.8%

IRR - Assuming 8.0x Entry Multiple

		Exit Year				
		2015	2016	2017	2018	2019
Exit Multiple	7.0x	14.5%	15.3%	15.1%	14.8%	14.5%
	7.5x	19.5%	18.6%	17.5%	16.6%	15.9%
	8.0x	24.1%	21.7%	19.7%	18.3%	17.2%
	8.5x	28.5%	24.6%	21.8%	19.9%	18.5%
	9.0x	32.5%	27.3%	23.8%	21.4%	19.7%

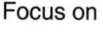

Step V: Perform LBO Analysis

Step V(c): Determine Valuation

- Sponsors base their LBO valuation in large part on their comfort with realizing acceptable returns at a given purchase price

($ in millions)

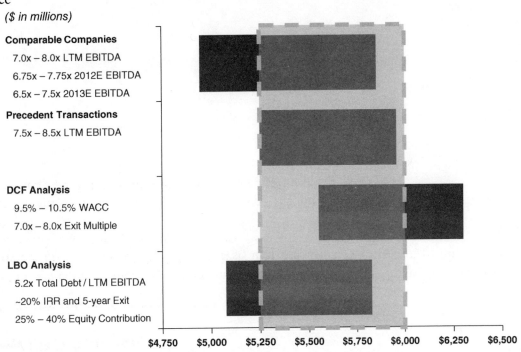

Comparable Companies

7.0x – 8.0x LTM EBITDA

6.75x – 7.75x 2012E EBITDA

6.5x – 7.5x 2013E EBITDA

Precedent Transactions

7.5x – 8.5x LTM EBITDA

DCF Analysis

9.5% – 10.5% WACC

7.0x – 8.0x Exit Multiple

LBO Analysis

5.2x Total Debt / LTM EBITDA

~20% IRR and 5-year Exit

25% – 40% Equity Contribution

$4,750 $5,000 $5,250 $5,500 $5,750 $6,000 $6,250 $6,500

Step V: Perform LBO Analysis

Step V(d): Create Transaction Summary Page

- Once the LBO model is fully functional, all the essential model outputs are linked to a transaction summary page
- This page provides an overview of the LBO analysis in a user-friendly format, typically displaying the sources and uses of funds, acquisition multiples, summary returns analysis, and summary financial data, as well as projected capitalization and credit statistics
- Allows the deal team to quickly review and spot-check the analysis and make adjustments to the purchase price, financing structure, operating assumptions, and other key inputs as necessary

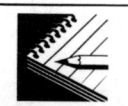

Step V: Perform LBO Analysis

ValueCo Corporation
Leveraged Buyout Analysis
($ in millions; fiscal year ending December 31)

Financing Structure: Structure 1
Operating Scenario: Base

Transaction Summary

Sources of Funds

	Amount	% of Total Sources	Multiple of EBITDA 9/30/2012	Cumulative	Pricing
Revolving Credit Facility	-	- %	- x	- x	L+425 bps
Term Loan A	-	- %	- x	- x	NA
Term Loan B	2,150.0	35.8%	3.1x	3.1x	L+450 bps
Term Loan C	-	- %	- x	3.1x	NA
2nd Lien	-	- %	- x	3.1x	NA
Senior Notes	1,500.0	25.0%	2.1x	5.2x	8.500%
Senior Subordinated Notes	-	- %	- x	5.2x	NA
Equity Contribution	2,100.0	35.0%	3.0x	8.2x	
Rollover Equity	-	- %	- x	8.2x	
Cash on Hand	250.0	4.2%	0.4x	8.6x	
Total Sources	**6,000.0**	**100.0%**	**8.6x**	**8.6x**	

Uses of Funds

	Amount	% of Total Uses
Purchase ValueCo Equity	4,350.0	72.5%
Repay Existing Net Debt	1,500.0	25.0%
Tender / Call Premiums	20.0	0.3%
Financing Fees	90.0	1.5%
Other Fees and Expenses	40.0	0.7%
Total Uses	**6,000.0**	**100.0%**

Purchase Price

Offer Price per Share	-
Fully Diluted Shares	-
Equity Purchase Price	4,350.0
Plus: Existing Net Debt	1,250.0
Enterprise Value	5,600.0

Transaction Multiples

Enterprise Value / Sales	
LTM 9/30/2012	3,385.0
2012E	3,450.0
Enterprise Value / EBITDA	
LTM 9/30/2012	700.0
2012E	725.0

Return Analysis

Exit Year	2017
Entry Multiple	8.0x
Exit Multiple	8.0x
IRR	20%
Cash Return	2.5x

Financing Structure / Options

Financing Structure	1
Operating Scenario	1
Cash Flow Sweep	1
Cash Balance	1
Average Interest	1
Financing Fees	1

Summary Financial Data

	Historical Period 2009	2010	2011	LTM 9/30/2012	Pro forma 2012	Year 1 2013	Year 2 2014	Year 3 2015	Year 4 2016	Year 5 2017	Year 6 2018	Year 7 2019	Year 8 2020	Year 9 2021	Year 10 2022
Sales	$2,600.0	$3,200.0	$3,200.0	$3,385.0	$3,450.0	$3,708.8	$3,931.3	$4,127.8	$4,293.0	$4,421.7	$4,554.4	$4,691.0	$4,831.8	$4,976.7	$5,126.0
% growth	NA	11.5%	10.3%	NA	7.8%	7.5%	6.0%	5.0%	4.0%	3.0%	3.0%	3.0%	3.0%	3.0%	3.0%
Gross Profit	$988.0	$1,131.0	$1,280.0	$1,350.0	$1,380.0	$1,483.5	$1,572.5	$1,651.1	$1,717.2	$1,768.7	$1,821.8	$1,876.4	$1,932.7	$1,990.7	$2,050.4
% margin	38.0%	39.0%	40.0%	39.9%	40.0%	40.0%	40.0%	40.0%	40.0%	40.0%	40.0%	40.0%	40.0%	40.0%	40.0%
EBITDA	$491.4	$580.0	$672.0	$700.0	$725.0	$779.4	$826.1	$867.4	$902.1	$929.2	$957.1	$985.8	$1,015.4	$1,045.8	$1,077.2
% margin	18.9%	20.0%	21.0%	20.7%	21.0%	21.0%	21.0%	21.0%	21.0%	21.0%	21.0%	21.0%	21.0%	21.0%	21.0%
Capital Expenditures	136.4	114.0	144.0	152.3	155.3	166.9	176.9	185.8	193.2	199.0	204.9	211.1	217.4	224.0	230.7
% sales	5.2%	3.9%	4.5%	4.5%	4.5%	4.5%	4.5%	4.5%	4.5%	4.5%	4.5%	4.5%	4.5%	4.5%	4.5%
Cash Interest Expense						252.5	246.6	233.7	218.7	201.7	182.8	163.6	141.2	128.9	128.9
Total Interest Expense						264.5	258.6	245.7	230.7	213.7	194.7	175.6	152.5	135.7	128.9
Free Cash Flow															
EBITDA						$779.4	$826.1	$867.4	$902.1	$929.2	$957.1	$985.8	$1,015.4	$1,045.8	$1,077.2
Less: Cash Interest Expense						(246.6)	(235.7)	(216.7)	(201.7)	(162.6)	(163.6)	(141.2)	(126.9)	(126.9)	(129.9)
Plus: Interest Income												1.1	3.2	5.4	
Less: Income Taxes						(118.3)	(130.9)	(147.8)	(163.7)	(179.3)	(193.1)	(209.7)	(224.5)	(236.2)	(245.5)
Less: Capital Expenditures						(166.9)	(176.9)	(185.8)	(193.2)	(199.0)	(204.9)	(211.1)	(217.4)	(224.0)	(230.7)
Less: Increase in Net Working Capital						(47.6)	(41.0)	(36.2)	(30.4)	(23.7)	(24.4)	(25.1)	(25.9)	(26.7)	(27.5)
Free Cash Flow						$204.9	$243.6	$278.9	$313.1	$345.5	$371.0	$398.7	$419.7	$433.3	$450.0
Cumulative Free Cash Flow						204.9	448.5	727.4	1,040.6	1,386.1	1,757.1	2,155.8	2,575.4	3,008.8	3,458.8

Capitalization

						Year 1	Year 2	Year 3	Year 4	Year 5	Year 6	Year 7	Year 8	Year 9	Year 10
Cash						-	-	-	-	-	5.8	425.4	858.8	1,308.8	
Revolving Credit Facility						-	-	-	-	-	-	-	-	-	
Term Loan A					2,150.0	1,945.1	1,701.5	1,422.6	1,109.4	763.9	392.9	-	-	-	
Term Loan B												-	-	-	
Term Loan C												-	-	-	
Existing Term Loan												-	-	-	
2nd Lien												-	-	-	
Other Debt												-	-	-	
Total Senior Secured Debt					$2,150.0	$1,945.1	$1,701.5	$1,422.6	$1,109.4	$763.9	$392.9	-	-	-	
Senior Notes					1,500.0	1,500.0	1,500.0	1,500.0	1,500.0	1,500.0	1,500.0	1,500.0	1,500.0	1,500.0	
Total Senior Debt					$3,650.0	$3,445.1	$3,201.5	$2,922.6	$2,609.4	$2,263.9	$1,892.9	$1,500.0	$1,500.0	$1,500.0	
Senior Subordinated Notes					-	-	-	-	-	-	-	-	-	-	
Total Debt					$3,650.0	$3,445.1	$3,201.5	$2,922.6	$2,609.4	$2,263.9	$1,892.9	$1,500.0	$1,500.0	$1,500.0	
Shareholders' Equity					2,040.0	2,224.9	2,438.5	2,679.7	2,946.9	3,297.8	3,552.9	3,895.6	4,261.4	4,646.7	5,047.3
Total Capitalization					$5,690.0	$5,670.0	$5,640.0	$5,602.3	$5,556.3	$5,561.6	$5,445.8	$5,395.6	$5,761.4	$6,146.7	$6,547.3
% of Bank Debt Repaid						9.5%	20.9%	33.8%	48.4%	64.5%	81.7%	100.0%	100.0%	100.0%	100.0%

Credit Statistics

						Year 1	Year 2	Year 3	Year 4	Year 5	Year 6	Year 7	Year 8	Year 9	Year 10
% Debt / Total Capitalization	64.1%	60.8%	56.8%	52.2%	47.0%	41.1%	34.8%	27.8%	26.0%	24.4%	22.9%				
EBITDA / Cash Interest Expense	2.9x	3.2x	3.5x	4.0x	4.5x	5.1x	5.8x	7.0x	7.9x	8.1x	8.4x				
(EBITDA - Capex) / Cash Interest Expense	2.3x	2.5x	2.8x	3.1x	3.5x	4.0x	4.6x	5.5x	6.2x	6.4x	6.6x				
EBITDA / Total Interest Expense	2.7x	3.0x	3.4x	3.8x	4.2x	4.8x	5.5x	6.5x	7.5x	8.1x	8.4x				
(EBITDA - Capex) / Total Interest Expense	2.2x	2.4x	2.6x	3.0x	3.3x	3.7x	4.3x	5.1x	5.9x	6.4x	6.6x				
Senior Secured Debt / EBITDA	3.0x	2.5x	2.1x	1.6x	1.2x	0.8x	0.4x	- x	- x	- x	- x				
Senior Debt / EBITDA	5.0x	4.4x	3.9x	3.4x	2.9x	2.4x	2.0x	1.5x	1.5x	1.4x	1.4x				
Total Debt / EBITDA	5.0x	4.4x	3.9x	3.4x	2.9x	2.4x	2.0x	1.5x	1.5x	1.4x	1.4x				
Net Debt / EBITDA	5.0x	4.4x	3.9x	3.4x	2.9x	2.4x	2.0x	1.5x	1.1x	0.6x	0.2x				

Chapter 6
Sell-Side M&A

Sell-Side M&A

Auctions
Organization and Preparation
First Round
Second Round
Negotiations
Closing
Negotiated Sale

Overview of Sell-Side M&A

- Sale of a company, division, business, or collection of assets ("target") is a major event for its owners (shareholders), management, employees, and other stakeholders
- Seller typically hires an investment bank and its team of trained professionals ("sell-side advisor") to ensure that key objectives are met and a favorable result is achieved
- Sell-side advisor seeks to achieve the optimal mix of *value maximization*, *speed of execution*, and *certainty of completion* among other deal-specific considerations for the selling party
- From an analytical perspective, a sell-side assignment requires the deal team to perform a comprehensive valuation of the target using those methodologies discussed in previous chapters
- For public targets (and certain private targets, depending on the situation) the sell-side advisor or an additional investment bank may be called upon to provide a fairness opinion

Valuation Paradigm

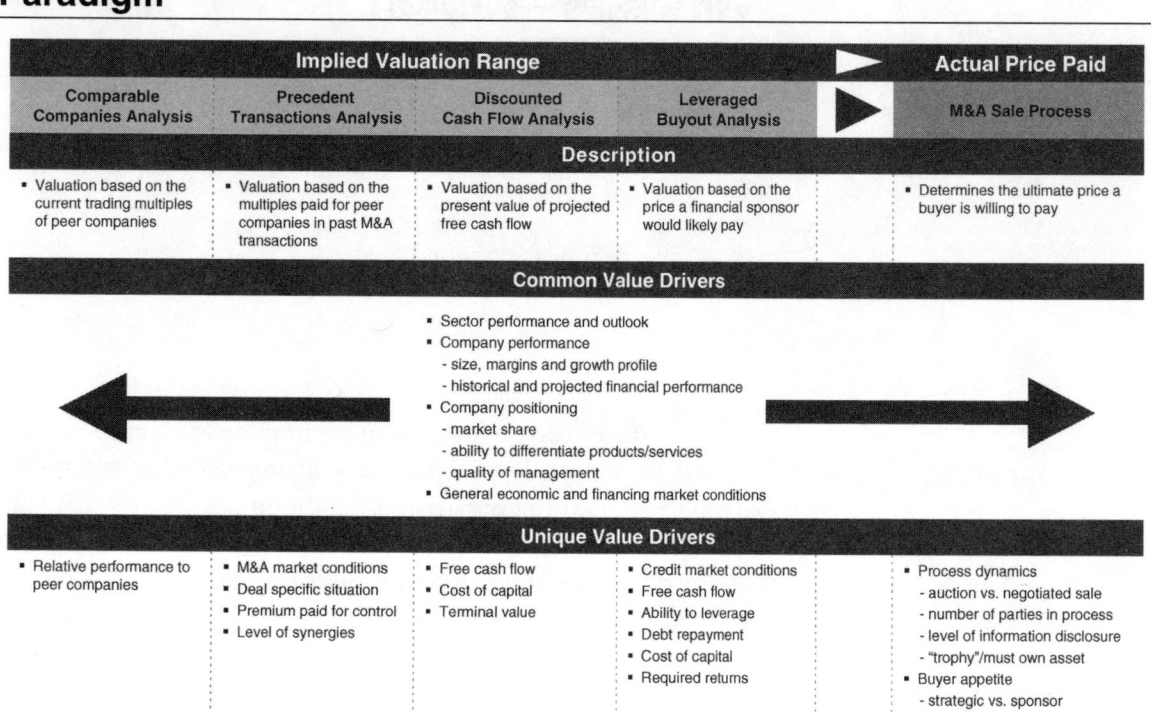

Implied Valuation Range				Actual Price Paid
Comparable Companies Analysis	**Precedent Transactions Analysis**	**Discounted Cash Flow Analysis**	**Leveraged Buyout Analysis**	**M&A Sale Process**
Description				
• Valuation based on the current trading multiples of peer companies	• Valuation based on the multiples paid for peer companies in past M&A transactions	• Valuation based on the present value of projected free cash flow	• Valuation based on the price a financial sponsor would likely pay	• Determines the ultimate price a buyer is willing to pay

Common Value Drivers

- Sector performance and outlook
- Company performance
  - size, margins and growth profile
  - historical and projected financial performance
- Company positioning
  - market share
  - ability to differentiate products/services
  - quality of management
- General economic and financing market conditions

Unique Value Drivers

• Relative performance to peer companies	• M&A market conditions
	• Deal specific situation
	• Premium paid for control
	• Level of synergies
		• Free cash flow
		• Cost of capital
		• Terminal value
			• Credit market conditions
			• Free cash flow
			• Ability to leverage
			• Debt repayment
			• Cost of capital
			• Required returns
				• Process dynamics
				  - auction vs. negotiated sale
				  - number of parties in process
				  - level of information disclosure
				  - "trophy"/must own asset
				• Buyer appetite
				  - strategic vs. sponsor
				  - desire/ability to pay
				  - amount needed to "win"
				• Pro forma impact to buyer
				  - financial effects
				  - pro forma leverage
				  - returns thresholds

Auctions

- An auction is a staged process whereby a target is marketed to multiple prospective buyers ("buyers" or "bidders")
- Provides a level of comfort that the market has been tested as well as a strong indicator of inherent value (supported by a fairness opinion, if required)
- May have potential drawbacks
  - Information leakage into the market from bidders
  - Negative impact on employee morale
  - Possible collusion among bidders
  - Reduced negotiating leverage once a "winner" is chosen (thereby encouraging re-trading)
  - "Taint" in the event of a failed auction
- Successful auction requires significant dedicated resources, experience, and expertise
  - Investment banks commit a team of bankers that is responsible for the day-to-day execution of the transaction
  - Also require significant time and attention from key members of the target's management team
- In the later stages of an auction, a senior member of the sell-side advisory team typically negotiates directly with prospective buyers with the goal of encouraging them to put forth their best offer
- Two types of auctions — Broad Auction and Targeted Auction

Auctions

Broad Auction

- Maximizes the universe of prospective buyers approached
- This involves contacting dozens of potential bidders, comprising both strategic buyers (potentially including direct competitors) and financial sponsors
- By casting as wide a net as possible, a broad auction is designed to maximize competitive dynamics, thereby increasing the likelihood of finding the best possible offer
- Typically involves more upfront organization and marketing due to the larger number of buyer participants in the early stages of the process

Targeted Auction

- Focuses on a few clearly defined buyers that have been identified as having a strong strategic fit and/or desire, as well as the financial capacity, to purchase the target
- More conducive to maintaining confidentiality and minimizing business disruption to the target
- Greater risk of "leaving money on the table" by excluding a potential bidder that may be willing to pay a higher price

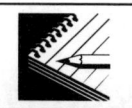

Auctions

Auction Structure

- Traditional auction is structured as a two-round bidding process that generally spans from three to six months (or longer) from the decision to sell until the signing of a definitive purchase/sale agreement ("definitive agreement") with the winning bidder
- Timing of the post signing ("closing") period depends on a variety of factors not specific to an auction, such as regulatory approvals and/or third-party consents, financing, and shareholder approval
- Entire auction process consists of multiple stages and discrete milestones within each of these stages

Auctions

Stages of an Auction Process				
Organization and Preparation	First Round	Second Round	Negotiations	Closing
▪ Identify seller objectives and determine appropriate sale process ▪ Perform sell-side advisor due diligence and preliminary valuation analysis ▪ Select buyer universe ▪ Prepare marketing materials ▪ Prepare confidentiality agreement	▪ Contact prospective buyers ▪ Negotiate and execute confidentiality agreements with interested parties ▪ Distribute CIM and initial bid procedures letter ▪ Prepare management presentation ▪ Set up data room ▪ Prepare stapled financing package (if applicable) ▪ Receive initial bids and select buyers to proceed to second round	▪ Conduct management presentations ▪ Facilitate site visits ▪ Provide data room access ▪ Distribute final bid procedures letter and draft definitive agreement ▪ Receive final bids	▪ Evaluate final bids ▪ Negotiate with preferred buyer(s) ▪ Select winning bidder ▪ Render fairness opinion (if required) ▪ Receive board approval and execute definitive agreement ("signing")	▪ Obtain necessary approvals ▪ Financing and closing
2 – 4 weeks	4 – 6 weeks	6 – 8 weeks	2 – 4 weeks (may include a third "mini round")	4 – 8 weeks +

Organization and Preparation

Identify Seller Objectives and Determine Appropriate Sale Process

Perform Sell-Side Advisor Due Diligence and Preliminary Valuation Analysis

Select Buyer Universe

Prepare Marketing Materials

Prepare Confidentiality Agreement

Organization and Preparation

Identify Seller Objectives and Determine Appropriate Sale Process

- At the onset of an auction, the sell-side advisor works with the seller to identify its objectives, determine the appropriate sale process to conduct, and develop a process roadmap
- Advisor must first gain a clear understanding of the seller's priorities so as to tailor the process accordingly
- Most basic decision is how many prospective buyers to approach (i.e., whether to run a broad or targeted auction)
- While a broad auction may be more appealing to a seller in certain circumstances, a targeted auction may better satisfy certain "softer" needs, such as speed to transaction closing, heightened confidentiality, and less risk of business disruption

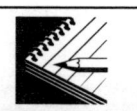

Organization and Preparation

Perform Sell-Side Advisor Due Diligence and Preliminary Valuation Analysis

- Sale process preparation begins with extensive due diligence on the part of the sell-side advisor
- Sell-side advisor must have a comprehensive understanding of the target's business and the management team's vision prior to drafting marketing materials and communicating with prospective buyers
- Due diligence facilitates the advisor's ability to properly position the target and articulate its investment merits
- A key portion of sell-side diligence centers on ensuring that the sell-side advisor understands and provides perspective on the assumptions that drive management's financial model
  - The model forms the basis for the valuation work that will be performed by prospective buyers
- An effective sell-side advisor understands the valuation methodologies that buyers will use in their analysis and performs this work beforehand to establish a valuation range benchmark
- In the event a *stapled financing package* is being provided, a separate financing deal team is formed (either at the sell-side advisor's institution or another bank) to begin conducting due diligence in parallel with the sell-side team

Organization and Preparation

Select Buyer Universe

- Selection of an appropriate group of prospective buyers, and compilation of corresponding contact information, is a critical part of the organization and preparation stage
- Omission or inclusion of a potential buyer (or buyers) can mean the difference between a successful or failed auction
- Sell-side advisors are selected on the basis of their sector knowledge, including their relationships with, and insights on, prospective buyers
- In a broad auction, the buyer list typically includes a mix of strategic buyers and financial sponsors
- When evaluating potential financial sponsor buyers, key criteria include investment strategy/focus, sector expertise, fund size, track record, fit within existing investment portfolio, fund life cycle, and ability to obtain financing
- In many cases, a strategic buyer is able to pay a higher price than a sponsor due to the ability to realize synergies and a lower cost of capital
- Once the sell-side advisor has compiled a list of prospective buyers, it presents them to the seller for final sign-off

Organization and Preparation

Prepare Marketing Materials

- Marketing materials often represent the first formal introduction of the target to prospective buyers
- Effective marketing materials present the target's investment highlights in a succinct manner, while also providing supporting evidence and basic operational, financial, and other essential business information
- Two main marketing documents for the first round of an auction process are the teaser and confidential information memorandum (CIM)

Teaser

- The teaser is the first marketing document presented to prospective buyers
- Designed to inform buyers and generate sufficient interest for them to do further work and potentially submit a bid
- Generally a brief one- or two-page synopsis of the target, including a company overview, investment highlights, and summary financial information

Organization and Preparation

Teaser

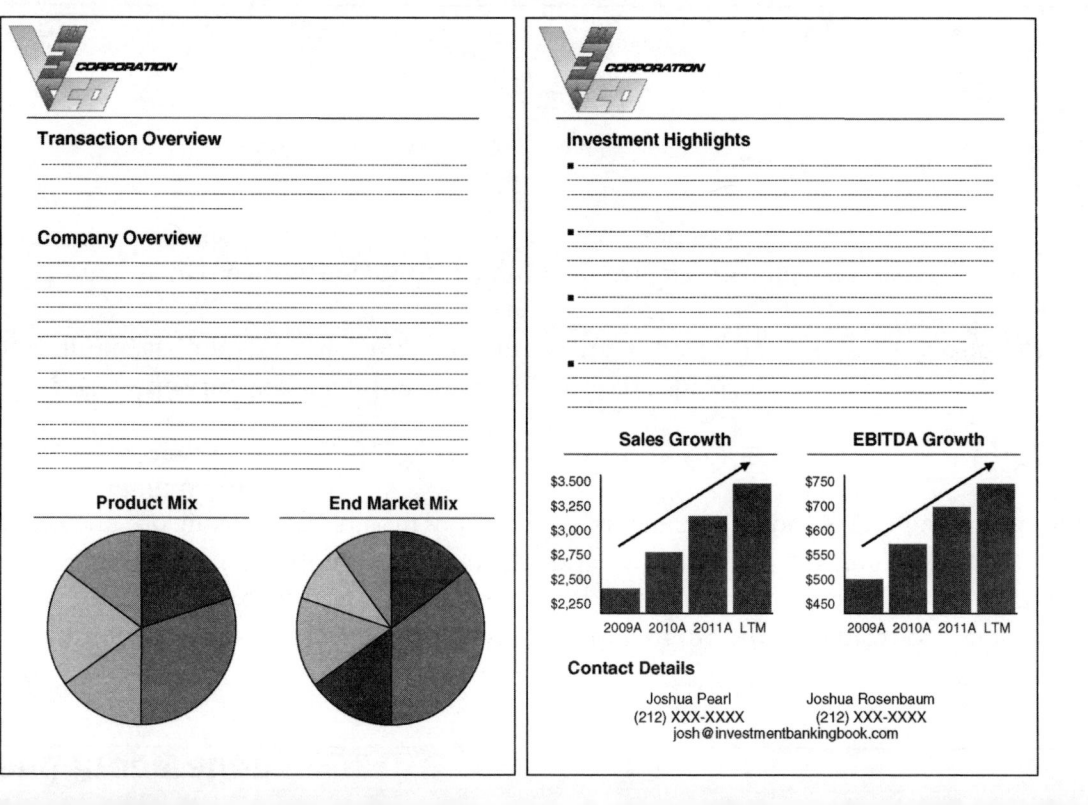

Organization and Preparation

Prepare Marketing Materials (continued)

Confidential Information Memorandum

- The CIM is a detailed written description of the target (often 50+ pages) that serves as the primary marketing document for the target in an auction
- The deal team, in collaboration with the target's management, spends significant time and resources drafting the CIM before it is deemed ready for distribution to prospective buyers
- Like teasers, CIMs vary in terms of format and content depending on situation-specific circumstances
- Financial information
  - CIM contains a detailed financial section presenting historical and projected financial information with accompanying narrative explaining both past and expected future performance (MD&A)
  - Involves normalizing the historical financials (e.g., for acquisitions, divestitures, and other one-time and/or extraordinary items) and crafting an accompanying MD&A
  - In some cases, the CIM provides additional financial information to help guide buyers toward potential growth/acquisition scenarios for the target

Organization and Preparation

Confidential Information Memorandum

Confidential Information Memorandum

Control Number 001

December 2012

Prepare Confidentiality Agreement

- A confidentiality agreement (CA) is a legally binding contract between the target and each prospective buyer that governs the sharing of confidential company information
- Drafted by the target's counsel and distributed to prospective buyers along with the teaser, with the understanding that the receipt of more detailed information is conditioned on execution of the CA
- Typical CA includes provisions governing the following:
  - Use of information
  - Term
  - Permitted disclosures
  - Return of confidential information
  - Non-solicitation/no hire
  - Standstill agreement
  - Restrictions on clubbing

First Round

Contact Prospective Buyers

Negotiate and Execute Confidentiality Agreements with Interested Parties

Distribute Confidential Information Memorandum and Initial Bid Procedures Letter

Prepare Management Presentation

Set up Data Room

Prepare Stapled Financing Package (if applicable)

Receive Initial Bids and Select Buyers to Proceed to Second Round

First Round

Contact Prospective Buyers

- The first round begins with the contacting of prospective buyers, which marks the formal launch of the auction process
- Typically takes the form of a scripted phone call to each prospective buyer by a senior member of the sell-side advisory team (and/or the coverage banker that maintains the relationship with the particular buyer), followed by the delivery of the teaser and CA
- Sell-side advisor generally keeps a detailed record of all interactions with prospective buyers, called a contact log, which is used as a tool to monitor a buyer's activity level and provide a record of the process

First Round

Negotiate and Execute Confidentiality Agreements with Interested Parties

- Upon receipt of the CA, a prospective buyer presents the document to its legal counsel for review
  - In the likely event there are comments, the buyer's counsel and seller's counsel negotiate the CA with input from their respective clients
- Following execution of the CA, the sell-side advisor is legally able to distribute the CIM and initial bid procedures letter to a prospective buyer
- Typical CA includes provisions governing the following:
  - *Use of information* – states that all information furnished by the seller, whether oral or written, is considered proprietary information and should be treated as confidential and used solely to make a decision regarding the proposed transaction
  - *Term* – designates the time period during which the confidentiality restrictions remain in effect
  - *Permitted disclosures* – outlines under what limited circumstances the prospective buyer is permitted to disclose the confidential information provided; also prohibits disclosure that the two parties are in negotiations
  - *Return of confidential information* – mandates return or destruction of all provided documents once prospective buyer exits process
  - *Non-solicitation/no hire* – prevents prospective buyers from soliciting to hire (or hiring) target employees for designated time period

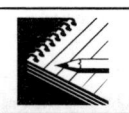

Negotiate and Execute Confidentiality Agreements with Interested Parties (continued)

- *Standstill agreement* – for public targets, precludes prospective buyers from making unsolicited offers or purchases of the target's shares, or seeking to control/influence the target's management, board of directors, or policies
- *Restrictions on clubbing* – prevents prospective buyers from collaborating with each other or with outside financial sponsors/equity providers without the prior consent of the target (in order to preserve a competitive environment)

First Round

Distribute Confidential Information Memorandum and Initial Bid Procedures Letter

- Prospective buyers are typically given several weeks to review the CIM, study the target and its sector, and conduct preliminary financial analysis prior to submitting their initial non-binding bids
- Depending on their level of interest, prospective buyers may also engage investment banks (as M&A buy-side advisors and/or financing providers), other external financing sources, and consultants at this stage
- Buy-side advisors play a critical role in helping their client, whether a strategic buyer or a financial sponsor, assess the target from a valuation perspective and determine a competitive initial bid price
- Financing sources help assess both the buyer's and target's ability to support a given capital structure and provide their clients with data points on amounts, terms, and availability of financing

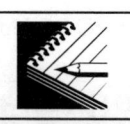

First Round

Distribute Confidential Information Memorandum and Initial Bid Procedures Letter (continued)

Initial Bid Procedures Letter

- Initial bid procedures letter states the date and time by which interested parties must submit their written, non-binding preliminary indications of interest ("first round bids")
- Also defines the exact information that should be included in the bid, such as
  - Indicative purchase price (typically presented as a range) and form of consideration (cash vs. stock mix)
  - Key assumptions to arrive at the stated purchase price
  - Structural and other considerations
  - Information on financing sources
  - Treatment of management and employees
  - Timing for completing a deal and diligence that must be performed
  - Key conditions to signing and closing
  - Required approvals
  - Buyer contact information

First Round

Prepare Management Presentation

- The management presentation is typically structured as a slideshow with accompanying hardcopy handout
- Sell-side advisor takes the lead on preparing these materials with substantial input from management
- The presentation format generally maps to that of the CIM, but is more crisp and concise

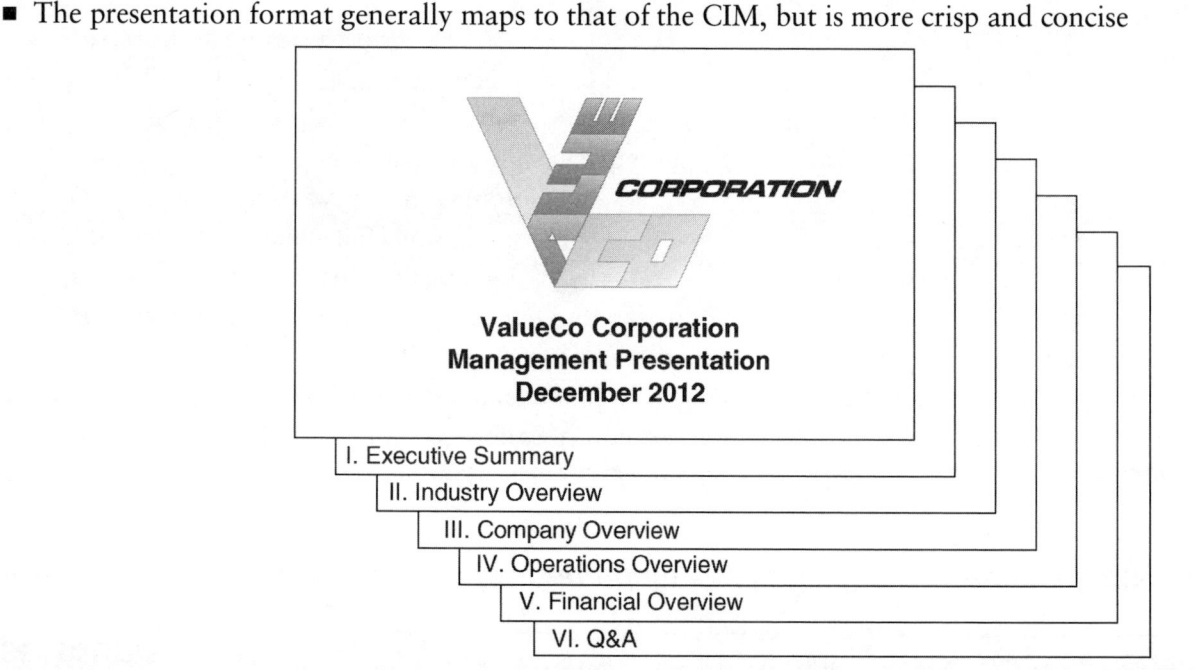

First Round

Set up Data Room

- The data room serves as the hub for the buyer due diligence that takes place in the second round of the process
  - It is a location, typically online, where comprehensive, detailed information about the target is stored, catalogued, and made available to pre-screened bidders
- Data rooms, such as those provided by Intralinks, generally contain a broad base of essential company information, documentation, and analyses
  - Also contains detailed company-specific information such as customer and supplier lists, labor contracts, purchase contracts, description and terms of outstanding debt, lease and pension contracts, and environmental compliance certification
- The data room also allows the buyer (together with its legal counsel, accountants, and other advisors) to perform more detailed confirmatory due diligence prior to consummating a transaction
- Sell-side bankers work closely with the target's legal counsel and selected employees to organize, populate, and manage the data room
- Access to the data room is typically granted to those buyers that move forward after first round bids, prior to, or coinciding with, their attendance at the management presentation

First Round

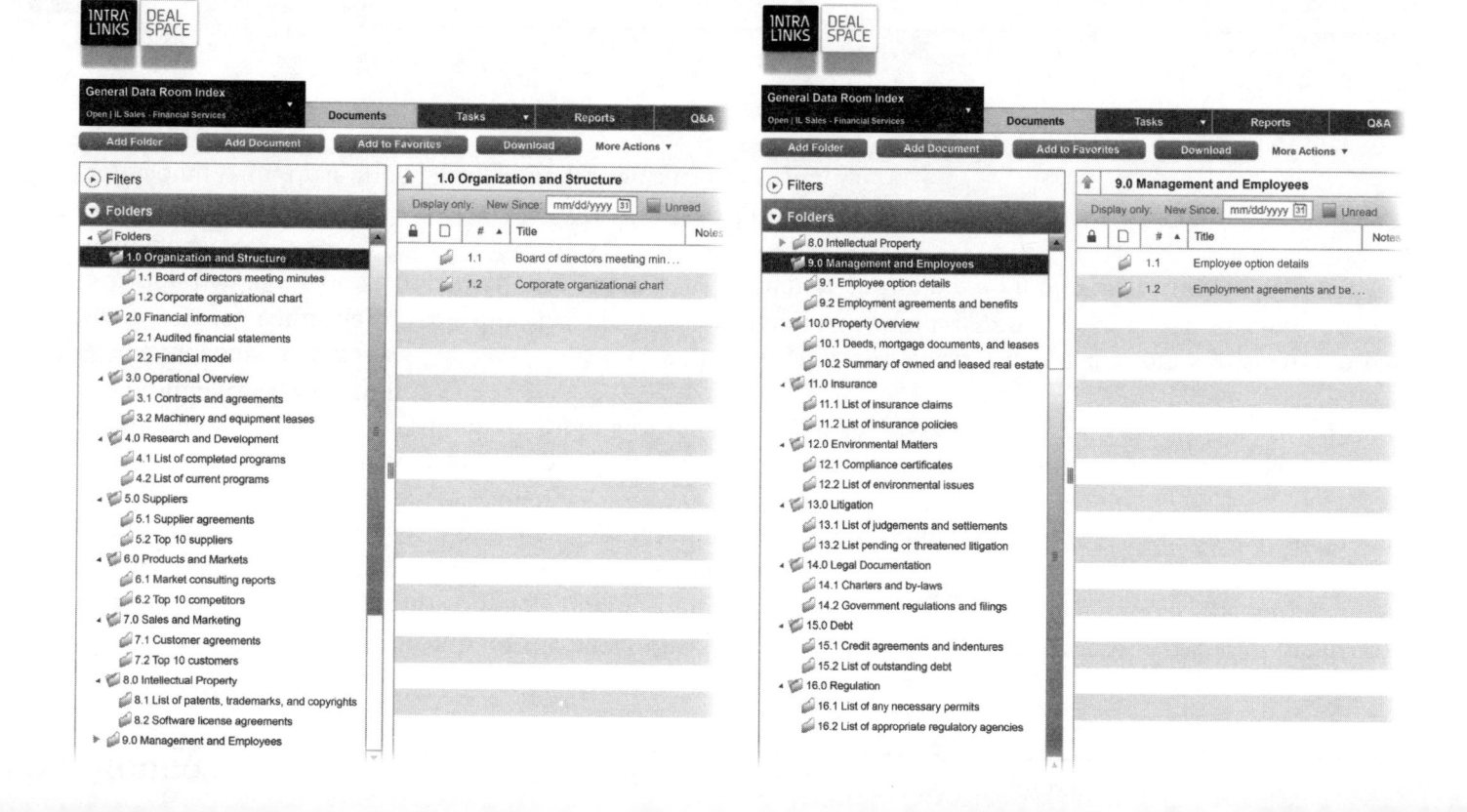

Prepare Stapled Financing Package (if applicable)

- The investment bank running the auction process (or sometimes a "partner" bank) may prepare a "pre-packaged" financing structure in support of the target being sold
  - For public companies, legal advisors need to be consulted before a sell-side advisor can be approved to provide a stapled financing
- Often, buyers seek their own financing sources to match or "beat" the staple
- To avoid a potential conflict of interest, the investment bank running the M&A sell-side sets up a separate financing team distinct from the sell-side advisory team to run the staple process
- The basic terms of the staple are typically communicated verbally to buyers in advance of the first round bid date so they can use that information to help frame their bids
- While buyers are not obligated to use the staple, it is designed to send a strong signal of support from the sell-side bank and provide comfort that the necessary financing will be available to buyers for the acquisition
- The staple may also compress the timing between the start of the auction's second round and signing of a definitive agreement by eliminating duplicate buyer financing due diligence

First Round

Receive Initial Bids and Select Buyers to Proceed to Second Round

- On the first round bid date, the sell-side advisor receives the initial indications of interest from prospective buyers
- An effective sell-side advisor is able to discern which bids are "real" (i.e., less likely to be re-traded)
- May also be dialogue with certain buyers at this point, typically focused on seeking clarification on key bid points
- Final decision regarding which buyers should advance, however, is made by the seller in consultation with its advisors

Second Round

Conduct Management Presentations

Facilitate Site Visits

Provide Data Room Access

Distribute Final Bid Procedures Letter and Draft Definitive Agreement

Receive Final Bids

Second Round

- Second round of the auction centers on facilitating the prospective buyers' ability to conduct detailed due diligence and analysis so they can submit strong, final (and ideally) binding bids by the set due date
- The diligence process is meant to be exhaustive, typically spanning several weeks, depending on the target's size, sector, geographies, and ownership
- Length and nature of the diligence process often differs based on the buyer's profile
- Sell-side advisor plays a central role during the second round by coordinating management presentations and facility site visits, monitoring the data room, and maintaining regular dialogue with prospective buyers
- Prospective buyers are given sufficient time to complete their due diligence, secure financing, craft a final bid price and structure, and submit a markup of the draft definitive agreement
- The sell-side advisor seeks to maintain a competitive atmosphere and keep the process moving by limiting the time available for due diligence, access to management, and ensuring bidders move in accordance with the established schedule

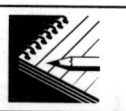

Second Round

Conduct Management Presentations

- The management presentation typically marks the formal kickoff of the second round, often spanning a full business day
- At the presentation, the target's management team presents each prospective buyer with a detailed overview of the company
- Core team presenting typically consists of the target's CEO, CFO, and key division heads or other operational executives, as appropriate
- Customary for prospective buyers to bring their investment banking advisors and financing sources, as well as industry and/or operational consultants, to the management presentation
- The management presentation is often the buyer's first meeting with management

Facilitate Site Visits

- Site visits are an essential component of buyer due diligence, providing a firsthand view of the target's operations
- Often, the management presentation itself takes place at, or near, a key company facility and includes a site visit as part of the agenda
- The typical site visit involves a guided tour of a key target facility, such as a manufacturing plant, distribution center, and/or sales office

Second Round

Provide Data Room Access

- The data room contains detailed information about all aspects of the target (e.g., business, financial, accounting, tax, legal, insurance, environmental, information technology, and property)
- Through rigorous data analysis and interpretation, the buyer seeks to identify the key opportunities and risks presented by the target, thereby framing the acquisition rationale and investment thesis
- Process also enables the buyer to identify those outstanding items and issues that should be satisfied prior to submitting a formal bid and/or specifically relating to the seller's proposed definitive agreement
- Data room access may be tailored to individual bidders or even specific members of the bidder teams (e.g., limited to legal counsel only)

Distribute Final Bid Procedures Letter and Draft Definitive Agreement

- During the second round, the final bid procedures letter is distributed to the remaining prospective buyers often along with the draft definitive agreement
- As part of their final bid package, prospective buyers submit a markup of the draft definitive agreement together with a cover letter detailing their proposal in response to the items outlined in the final bid procedures letter

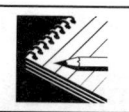

Distribute Final Bid Procedures Letter and Draft Definitive Agreement (continued)

Final Bid Procedures Letter

- The final bid procedures letter outlines the exact date and guidelines for submitting a final, legally binding bid package
- Requirements for the final bid are stringent:
  - Purchase price details, including the exact dollar amount of the offer and form of purchase consideration (e.g., cash vs. stock)
  - Markup of the draft definitive agreement provided by the seller in a form that the buyer would be willing to sign
  - Evidence of committed financing and information on financing sources
  - Attestation to completion of due diligence (or very limited confirmatory due diligence required)
  - Attestation that the offer is binding and will remain open for a designated period of time
  - Required regulatory approvals and timeline for completion
  - Board of directors approvals (if appropriate)
  - Estimated time to sign and close the transaction
  - Buyer contact information

Second Round

Distribute Final Bid Procedures Letter and Draft Definitive Agreement (continued)

Definitive Agreement

- The definitive agreement is a legally binding contract between buyer and seller detailing the terms and conditions of the sale transaction
- Distributed to prospective buyers (and their legal counsel) during the second round—often toward the end of the diligence process
- Ideally, the buyer is required to submit a form of revised definitive agreement that it would be willing to sign immediately if the bid is accepted
- Definitive agreements involving public and private companies differ in terms of content, although the basic format of the document is the same
  - Overview of the transaction structure/deal mechanics
  - Representations and warranties
  - Pre-closing commitments (including covenants)
  - Closing conditions
  - Termination provisions
  - Indemnities (if applicable)
  - Associated disclosure schedules and exhibits

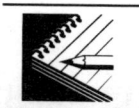

Second Round

Receive Final Bids

- Upon conclusion of the second round, prospective buyers submit their final bid packages to the sell-side advisor by the date indicated in the final bid procedures letter
- These bids are expected to be final with minimal conditionality, or "outs," such as the need for additional due diligence or firming up of financing commitments
- In practice, the sell-side advisor works with viable buyers throughout the second round to firm up their bids as much as possible before submission

Negotiations

Evaluate Final Bids

Negotiate with Preferred Buyer(s)

Select Winning Bidder

Render Fairness Opinion (if required)

Receive Board Approval and Execute Definitive Agreement

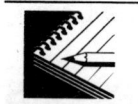

Negotiations

Evaluate Final Bids

- The sell-side advisor works together with the seller and its legal counsel to conduct a thorough analysis of the price, structure, and conditionality of the final bids
- Purchase price is assessed within the context of the first round bids and the target's recent financial performance, as well as the valuation work performed by the sell-side advisors
- The deemed binding nature of each final bid, or lack thereof, is also carefully weighed in assessing its strength

Negotiate with Preferred Buyer(s)

- Often, the sell-side advisor recommends that the seller negotiates with two (or more) parties, especially if the bid packages are relatively close
- Advisor seeks to maintain a level playing field so as not to advantage one bidder over another and maximize the competitiveness of the final stage of the process
- During these final negotiations, the advisor works intensely with the bidders to clear away any remaining confirmatory diligence items (if any)

Negotiations

Select Winning Bidder

- The sell-side advisor and legal counsel negotiate a final definitive agreement with the winning bidder, which is then presented to the target's board of directors for approval
- Seller normally reserves the right to reject any and all bids as inadequate at every stage of the process
- Each prospective buyer has the right to withdraw from the process at any time prior to the execution of a binding definitive agreement
- Not all auctions result in a successful sale

Render Fairness Opinion

- In response to a proposed offer for a public company, the target's board of directors typically requires a fairness opinion to be rendered as one item for their consideration before making a recommendation on whether to accept the offer and approve the execution of a definitive agreement
- A fairness opinion is a letter opining on the "fairness" (from a financial point of view) of the consideration offered in a transaction
- Opinion letter is supported by detailed analysis and documentation providing an overview of the sale process run (including number of parties contacted and range of bids received), as well as an objective valuation of the target
- Prior to the delivery of the fairness opinion to the board of directors, the sell-side advisory team must receive approval from its internal fairness opinion committee
- In a public deal, the fairness opinion and supporting analysis is publicly disclosed and described in detail in the relevant SEC filings

Negotiations

Receive Board Approval and Execute Definitive Agreement

- Once the seller's board of directors votes to approve the deal, the definitive agreement is executed by the buyer and seller
- A formal transaction announcement agreed to by both parties is made with key deal terms disclosed depending on the situation
- The two parties then proceed to satisfy all of the closing conditions to the deal, including regulatory and shareholder approvals

Closing

Obtain Necessary Approvals

Financing and Closing

Closing

Obtain Necessary Approvals

Regulatory Approval

- The primary regulatory approval requirement for the majority of U.S. M&A transactions is made in accordance with the Hart-Scott-Rodino Antitrust Improvements Act of 1976 (the "HSR Act")
- Depending on the size of the transaction, the HSR Act requires both parties to an M&A transaction to file respective notifications and report forms with the Federal Trade Commission (FTC) and Antitrust Division of the Department of Justice (DOJ)
  - Companies with significant foreign operations may require approval from comparable foreign regulatory authorities such as the Competition Bureau (Canada) and European Commission (European Union)
- The HSR filing is typically made directly following the execution of a definitive agreement

Closing

Obtain Necessary Approvals (continued)

Shareholder Approval: One-Step Merger

- In a "one-step" merger transaction for public companies, target shareholders vote on whether to approve or reject the proposed transaction at a formal shareholder meeting pursuant to relevant state law
- Shareholder approval is typically determined by a majority vote, or 50.1% of the voting stock
- In a one-step merger, the timing from the signing of a definitive agreement to closing may take as little as six weeks, but often takes longer (perhaps three or four months) depending on the size and complexity of the transaction
- Main driver of the timing is the SEC's decision on whether to comment on the public disclosure documents
- Following the SEC's approval, the documents are mailed to shareholders and a meeting is scheduled to approve the deal, which typically adds a month or more to the timetable

Closing

Obtain Necessary Approvals (continued)

Shareholder Approval: Two-Step Tender Process

- Alternatively, a public acquisition can be structured as a "two-step" tender offer on either a negotiated or unsolicited basis, followed by a merger
- In Step I of the two-step process, the tender offer is made directly to the target's public shareholders with the target's approval pursuant to a definitive agreement
  - The tender offer is conditioned, among other things, on sufficient acceptances to ensure that the buyer will acquire a majority (or supermajority, as appropriate) of the target's shares within 20 business days of launching the offer
- If the buyer only succeeds in acquiring a majority (or supermajority, as appropriate) of the shares in the tender offer, it would then have to complete the shareholder meeting and approval mechanics in accordance with a "one-step" merger (with approval assured because of the buyer's majority ownership)
- If the requisite threshold of tendered shares is reached as designed (typically 90%), the acquirer can subsequently consummate a back-end "short form" merger (Step II) to squeeze out the remaining public shareholders without needing to obtain shareholder approval
- In a squeeze out scenario, entire process can be completed much quicker than a one-step merger; few as five weeks
- If the buyer needs to access the public capital markets to finance the transaction, the timing advantage of a tender offer would most likely be lost as such transactions typically take approximately 75 to 90 days to arrange post-signing

Closing

Financing and Closing

- In parallel with obtaining all necessary approvals and consents as defined in the definitive agreement, the buyer proceeds to source the necessary capital to fund and close the transaction
- Financing process timing may range from relatively instantaneous (e.g., the buyer has necessary cash-on-hand or revolver availability) to several weeks or months for funding that requires access to the capital markets (e.g., bank, bond, and/or equity financing)
  - In the latter scenario, the buyer begins the marketing process for the financing following the signing of the definitive agreement so as to be ready to fund expeditiously once all of the conditions to closing in the definitive agreement are satisfied
  - Acquirer may also use bridge financing to fund and close the transaction prior to raising permanent debt or equity capital
- Once the financing is received and conditions to closing in the definitive agreement are met, the transaction is funded and closed

Negotiated Sale

- While auctions were prevalent as a sell-side mechanism during the LBO boom of the mid-2000s, a substantial portion of M&A activity is conducted through negotiated transactions
- In contrast to an auction, a negotiated sale centers on a direct dialogue with a single prospective buyer
- Negotiated sales are particularly compelling in situations involving a natural strategic buyer with clear synergies and strategic fit
- In many negotiated sales, the banker plays a critical role as the idea generator and/or intermediary before a formal process begins
- Many of the key negotiated sale process points mirror those of an auction, but on a compressed timetable
- In some cases, a negotiated sale may move faster than an auction as much of the upfront preparation, buyer contact, and marketing is bypassed
- Ideally the seller realizes fair and potentially full value for the target while avoiding the potential risks and disadvantages of an auction

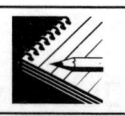

Chapter 7
Buy-Side M&A

Overview of Buy-Side M&A

- Mergers and acquisitions ("M&A") is a catch-all phrase for the purchase, sale, and combination of companies, their subsidiaries and assets
  - Facilitates a company's ability to continuously grow, evolve, and re-focus in accordance with ever-changing market conditions, industry trends, and shareholder demands
- In strong economic times, M&A activity tends to increase as company management confidence is high and financing is readily available
- In more difficult times, M&A activity typically slows down as financing becomes more expensive and buyers focus on their core businesses, as well as fortifying their balance sheet
- M&A transactions, including LBOs, tend to be the highest profile part of investment banking activity, with larger, "big name" deals receiving a great deal of media attention
- For the companies and key executives involved, the decision to buy, sell, or combine with another company is usually a transformational event
- Investment banking advisory assignment for a company seeking to buy another company, or part thereof, is referred to as a "buy-side" assignment

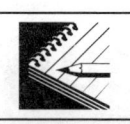

Overview of Buy-Side M&A

- Core analytical work on buy-side advisory engagements centers on the construction of a detailed financial model
  - Used to assess valuation, financing structure, and financial impact to the acquirer ("merger consequences analysis")
- Banker also advises on key process tactics and strategy, and plays the lead role in interfacing with the seller and its advisor(s)
  - Buy-side adviser is trusted with outmaneuvering other bidders while not exceeding the client's ability to pay
  - Bankers are typically chosen for their prior deal experience, negotiating skills, and deal-making ability, in addition to technical expertise, sector knowledge, and relationships
- For day-to-day execution, an appointed member(s) of the investment banking advisory team liaises with a point person(s) at the client company (e.g., a key executive or someone from its corporate development group)
  - Client point person is charged with corralling internal resources as appropriate to ensure a smooth and timely process
  - Company input is essential for performing mergers consequences analysis, including determining synergies and conducting EPS accretion/(dilution) and balance sheet effects

Buyer Motivation

- Decision to buy another company (or assets of another company) is driven by numerous factors, including the desire to grow, improve, and/or expand an existing business platform
  - Growth through an acquisition represents a cheaper, faster, and less risky option than building a business from scratch
  - *Greenfielding* a new facility, expanding into a new geographic region, and/or moving into a new product line or distribution channel is typically more risky, costly, and time-consuming than buying an existing company with an established business model, infrastructure, and customer base
- Successful acquirers are capable of fully integrating newly purchased companies quickly and efficiently with minimal disruption to the existing business
- Acquisitions typically build upon a company's core business strengths with the goal of delivering growth and enhanced profitability to provide higher returns to shareholders
  - May be undertaken directly within an acquirer's existing product lines, geographies, or other core competencies (often referred to as "bolt-on acquisitions"), or represent an extension into new focus areas
- For acquisitions within core competencies, acquirers seek value creation opportunities from combining the businesses, such as cost savings and enhanced growth initiatives
  - Acquirers need to be mindful of abiding by anti-trust legislation that prevents them from gaining too much share in a given market, thereby creating potential monopoly effects and restraining competition

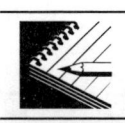

Buyer Motivation

Synergies

- Synergies refer to expected cost savings, growth opportunities, and other financial benefits that occur as a result of the combination of two companies
- Size and degree of likelihood for realizing potential synergies plays an important role in framing purchase price
- Buy-side deal team must ensure that synergies are accurately reflected in the financial model and M&A analysis, as well as in communication to the public markets
- Upon announcement of a material acquisition, public acquirers typically provide the investor community with guidance on expected synergies
- Successful and timely delivery of expected synergies is extremely important for the acquirer and, in particular, the executive management team
- Synergies tend to be greater, and the degree of success higher, when acquirers buy targets in the same or closely-related businesses

Buyer Motivation

Synergies (continued)

- Cost synergies, which are easily quantifiable (such as headcount reduction and facility consolidation), tend to have a higher likelihood of success than revenue synergies
- Other synergies may include tangible financial benefits such as adopting the target's net operating losses (NOLs) for tax purposes, or a lower cost of capital due to the increased size, diversification, and market share of the combined entity

Cost Synergies

- Traditional synergies include headcount reduction, consolidation of overlapping facilities, and the ability to buy key inputs at lower prices due to increased purchasing power
- Increased size enhances a company's ability to leverage its fixed cost base (e.g., administrative overhead, marketing and advertising expenses) across existing and new products, as well as to obtain better terms from suppliers due to larger volume orders, also known as "purchasing synergies"
- Another common cost synergy is the adoption of "best practices"

Buyer Motivation

Revenue Synergies

- Revenue synergies refer to the enhanced sales growth opportunities presented by the combination of businesses
- Typical revenue synergy is the acquirer's ability to sell the target's products though its own distribution channels without cannibalizing existing acquirer or target sales
- An additional revenue synergy occurs when the acquirer leverages the target's technology, geographic presence, or know-how to enhance or expand its existing product or service offering
- Revenues synergies tend to be more speculative than cost synergies

Acquisition Strategies

- Companies are guided by a variety of acquisition strategies in their pursuit of growth and enhanced profitability
- The two most common frameworks for viewing acquisition strategies are horizontal and vertical integration
  - Horizontal integration is the acquisition of a company at the same level of the value chain as the acquirer
  - Vertical integration occurs when a company either expands upstream in the supply chain by acquiring an existing or potential supplier, or downstream by acquiring an existing or potential customer
- Alternatively, some companies make acquisitions in relatively unrelated business areas, an acquisition strategy known as conglomeration
  - In so doing, they compile a portfolio of disparate businesses under one management team, typically with the goal of providing an attractive investment vehicle for shareholders while diversifying risk

Acquisition Strategies

Horizontal Integration

- Horizontal integration involves the purchase of a business that expands the acquirer's geographic reach, product lines, services, or distribution channels
- Often results in significant cost synergies from eliminating redundancies and leveraging the acquirer's existing infrastructure and overhead
- A horizontal acquisition strategy typically also provides synergy opportunities from leveraging each respective company's distribution network, customer base, and technologies
- A thoughtful horizontal integration strategy tends to produce higher synergy realization and shareholder returns than acquisitions of relatively unrelated businesses
- While the acquirer's internal M&A team or operators take the lead on formulating synergy estimates, bankers are often called upon to provide input

Acquisition Strategies

Vertical Integration

- Vertical integration seeks to provide a company with cost efficiencies and potential growth opportunities by affording control over key components of the supply chain
- When companies move upstream to purchase their suppliers, it is known as backward integration
  - An automobile original equipment manufacturer (OEM) moving upstream to acquire an axle manufacturer or steel producer is an example of backward integration
- When companies move downstream to purchase their customers, it is known as forward integration
  - An example of forward integration would involve an OEM moving downstream to acquire a distributor

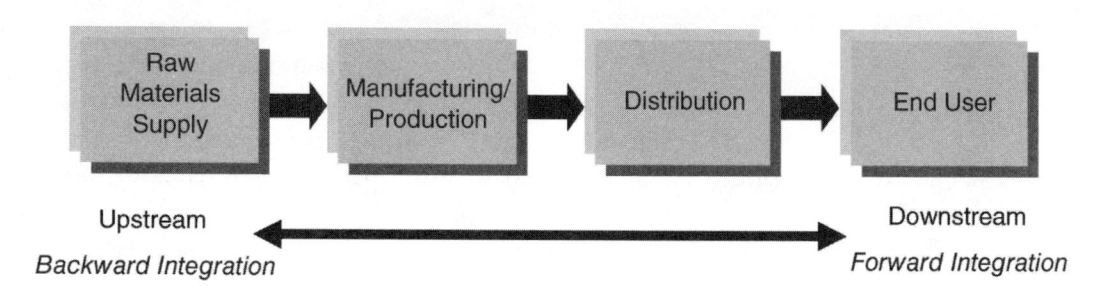

Acquisition Strategies

Vertical Integration (continued)

- Vertical integration is motivated by a multitude of potential advantages
  - Increased control over key raw materials and other essential inputs
  - Ability to capture upstream or downstream profit margins
  - Improved supply chain coordination
  - Moving closer to the end user to "own" the customer relationship

Acquisition Strategies

Conglomeration

- Conglomeration refers to a strategy that brings together companies that are generally unrelated in terms of products and services provided under one corporate umbrella
- Conglomerates tend to be united in their business approach and use of best practices, as well as the ability to leverage a common management team infrastructure and balance sheet to benefit a broad range of businesses
  - Conglomeration strategy also seeks to benefit from portfolio diversification benefits while affording the flexibility to opportunistically invest in higher growth segments
- Two of the largest and most well-known conglomerates are General Electric ("GE") and Berkshire Hathaway ("Berkshire")
  - GE operates a variety of businesses in several sectors including aerospace, energy, financial and insurance services, healthcare, and transportation
  - Like GE, Berkshire is engaged in a number of diverse business activities including insurance, apparel, building products, chemicals, energy, general industrial, retail, and transportation
  - Investors in GE and Berkshire believe that management competency, business practices, philosophy, and investment strategies at these companies add tangible value

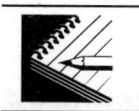

Form of Financing

- Form of financing refers to sourcing of internal and/or external capital used as consideration to fund an M&A transaction
- Form of financing directly drives certain parts of merger consequences analysis; thereby affecting the amount an acquirer is willing to or can afford to pay for the target
- Sellers may have preference for certain type of consideration (e.g., cash over stock) that may affect their perception of value
- Form of financing available to acquirer is dependent upon several factors, including its size, balance sheet, and credit profile
- Acquirer typically chooses among the available sources of funds based on a variety of factors, including cost of capital, balance sheet flexibility, rating agency considerations, and speed and certainty to close the transaction
- Cash on hand and debt financing are often viewed as equivalent, and both are cheaper than equity
- Bankers play an important role in advising companies on their financing options and optimal structure in terms of type of securities, leverage levels, cost, and flexibility

Form of Financing

Cash on Hand

- Use of cash on hand pertains to strategic buyers that employ excess cash on their balance sheet to fund acquisitions
  - Nominally, it is the cheapest form of acquisition financing as its cost is simply the foregone interest income earned on the cash, which is minimal in a low interest rate environment
  - In practice, however, companies tend to view use of cash in terms of the opportunity cost of raising external debt as cash can theoretically be used to repay existing debt
- As a general rule, companies do not rely upon the maintenance of a substantial cash position (also referred to as a "war chest") to fund sizeable acquisitions
  - Instead, they tend to access the capital markets when attractive acquisition opportunities are identified
  - Large portion of a company's cash position may be held outside of the United States and face substantial tax repatriation expenses, thereby limiting its availability for domestic M&A opportunities

Form of Financing

Debt Financing

- Refers to the issuance of new debt or use of revolver availability to partially, or fully, fund an M&A transaction
- Revolving credit facility
  - Essentially a line of credit extended by a bank or group of banks that permits the borrower to draw varying amounts up to a specified limit for a specified period of time
- Term loan
  - Loan for a specific period of time that requires principal repayment ("amortization") according to defined schedule, typically on quarterly basis
  - Revolvers and term loans bear interest on quarterly basis at floating rate, based on underlying benchmark (typically LIBOR), plus applicable margin
- Bond or note
  - Security that obligates the issuer to pay bondholders interest payments at regularly defined intervals (typically cash payments on a semi-annual basis at a fixed rate) and repay the entire principal at a stated maturity date

Form of Financing

Debt Financing (continued)

- Commercial Paper
  - Short-term (typically less than 270 days), unsecured corporate debt instrument issued by investment-grade companies for near-term use
  - Typically issued as a zero coupon instrument at a discount, like T-bills
- All-in cost of debt must be viewed on a tax-effected basis as interest payments are tax deductible
- Acquirers are constrained with regard to the amount of debt they can incur in terms of covenants, market permissiveness, and credit ratings, as well as balance sheet flexibility considerations

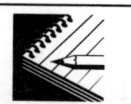

Form of Financing

Equity Financing

- Refers to a company's use of its stock as acquisition currency; mainstay of M&A financing particularly for large-scale public transactions
- Acquirer can either offer its own stock directly to target shareholders as purchase consideration or offer cash proceeds from an equity offering
- Equity financing provides issuers with greater flexibility as there are no mandatory cash interest payments (dividends are discretionary), no principal repayment, and no covenants
- Acquirers are more inclined to use equity when their share price is high, both on an absolute basis and relative to that of the target
- From a target company perspective, shareholders may find stock compensation attractive provided that the acquirer's shares are perceived to have upside potential (including synergies from the contemplated deal)
- More commonly, however, target shareholders view equity as a less desirable form of compensation than cash

Deal Structure

- As with form of financing, detailed valuation and merger consequences analysis requires the banker to make initial assumptions regarding deal structure
- Deal structure pertains to how the transaction is legally structured, such as a Stock Sale (including a 338(h)(10) Election) or an Asset Sale
- For the buyer, it is a key component in valuation and merger consequences analysis, and therefore affects willingness and ability to pay
- For the seller, it can have a direct impact on after-tax proceeds

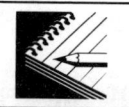

Deal Structure

Stock Sale

- Stock sale is most common form of M&A deal structure, particularly for C Corporation (also known as a "C Corp")
  - C Corp is a corporation that is taxed separately from its shareholders (i.e., at the corporate level only as opposed to the shareholder level)
  - S Corps, LLCs or other partnerships, by contrast, are conduit entities in which corporate earnings are passed on directly to shareholders and therefore not taxed at the corporate level
- Stock sale involves the acquirer purchasing target's stock from the company's shareholders for some form of consideration
  - From a tax perspective, in the event that target shareholders receive significant equity consideration in the acquirer, their capital gain is generally deferred
  - In the event they receive cash, a capital gain is triggered
  - Extent to which a capital gains tax is triggered is dependent upon whether the shareholder is taxable (e.g., an individual) or non-taxable (e.g., a pension fund)
- Target ceases to remain in existence post-transaction in stock sale, becoming wholly-owned subsidiary acquirer
  - Acquirer assumes all of the target's past, present, and future known and unknown liabilities, in addition to the assets
  - Stock sale is the cleanest form of transaction from the seller's perspective, eliminating all tail liabilities

Deal Structure

Stock Sale (continued)

Goodwill

- In modeling a stock sale transaction for financial accounting (GAAP) purposes, in the event the purchase price exceeds the net identifiable assets of the target, the excess is first allocated to the target's tangible and identifiable intangible assets, which are "written-up" to their fair market value
  - As their respective names connote, tangible assets refer to "hard" assets such as PP&E and inventory, while intangibles refer to items such as customer lists, non-compete contracts, copyrights, and patents
- These tangible and intangible asset write-ups are reflected in the acquirer's pro forma GAAP balance sheet
  - They are then depreciated and amortized, respectively, over their useful lives, thereby reducing after-tax GAAP earnings
  - For modeling purposes, simplifying assumptions are typically made regarding the amount of the write-ups to the target's tangible and intangible assets before the receipt of more detailed information
- In a stock sale, the transaction-related depreciation and amortization is not deductible for tax purposes
- Neither buyer nor seller pays taxes on the "gain" on the GAAP asset write-up
  - From an IRS tax revenue generation standpoint, the buyer should not be allowed to reap future tax deduction benefits from this accounting convention
- From an accounting perspective, this discrepancy between book and tax is resolved through the creation of a deferred tax liability (DTL) on the balance sheet (where it often appears as deferred income taxes)

Deal Structure

Stock Sale (continued)

Goodwill

- Goodwill is calculated as purchase price minus target's net identifiable assets after allocations to the target's tangible and intangible assets
- Once calculated, goodwill is added to the assets side of the acquirer's balance sheet and tested annually for impairment, with certain exceptions
- A graphical representation of calculation of goodwill, including asset write-up and DTL adjustments, is shown below

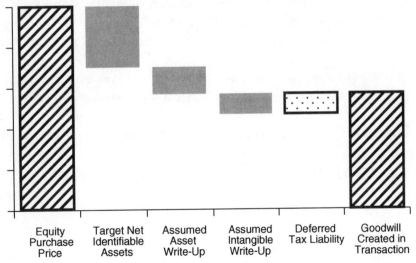

Deal Structure

Stock Sale (continued)

Deferred Tax Liability (DTL)

- DTL is created due to the fact that the target's written-up assets are depreciated on a GAAP book basis but not for tax purposes
  - While depreciation expense is netted out from pre-tax income on GAAP income statement, company does not receive cash benefits from tax shield
  - Perceived tax shield on the book depreciation exists for accounting purposes only
  - In reality, company must pay cash taxes on pre-tax income amount before the deduction of transaction-related depreciation and amortization expense
- DTL line item on the balance sheet remedies this accounting discrepancy between book basis and tax basis
  - Serves as a reserve account that is reduced annually by the amount of the taxes associated with the new transaction-related depreciation and amortization (i.e., the annual depreciation and amortization amounts multiplied by the company's tax rate)
  - Annual tax payment is a real use of cash and runs through the company's statement of cash flows

Deal Structure

Stock Sale (continued)

Goodwill

- The DTL is calculated as the amount of the asset write-up multiplied by the company's tax rate

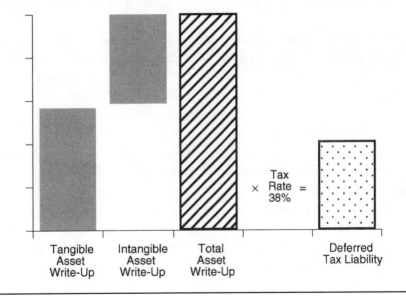

Deal Structure

Asset Sale

- An asset sale refers to an M&A transaction whereby an acquirer purchases all or some of the target's assets
- Target legally remains in existence post-transaction, which means that the buyer purchases specified assets and assumes certain liabilities
  - Can help alleviate buyer's risk, especially when there may be substantial unknown contingent liabilities
  - From the seller's perspective this is often less attractive than a stock sale where liabilities are transferred as part of the deal and the seller is absolved from all liabilities, including potential contingent liabilities
  - Complete asset sale for a public company is a rare event
- An asset sale may provide certain tax benefits for the buyer in the event it can "step up" the tax basis of the target's acquired assets to fair market value, as reflected in the purchase price
  - Stepped-up portion is depreciable and/or amortizable on a tax deductible basis over the assets' useful life for both GAAP book and tax purposes
  - Results in real cash benefits for the buyer during the stepped-up depreciable period
- First level of taxation occurs at the corporate level, where taxes on the gain upon sale of the assets are paid at the corporate income rate
- Second level of taxation takes place upon distribution of proceeds to shareholders in the form of a capital gains tax on the gain in the appreciation of their stock

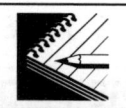

Deal Structure

Asset Sale (continued)

- Upfront double taxation hit to the seller in an asset sale tends to outweigh the tax shield benefits to the buyer, which are realized over an extended period of time
  - Hence, stock deals are the most common structure for C Corps
- In deciding upon an asset sale or stock sale from a pure after-tax proceeds perspective, the seller also considers the tax basis of its assets (also known as "inside basis") and stock (also known as "outside basis")
- In the event the company has a lower inside basis than outside basis, which is commonplace, the result is a larger gain upon sale
  - This would further encourage the seller to eschew an asset sale in favor of a stock sale due to the larger tax burden
  - As a result, asset sales are most attractive for subsidiary sales when the parent company seller has significant losses or other tax attributes to shield the corporate-level tax
  - Eliminates double taxation for the seller while affording the buyer the tax benefits of the step-up
- An asset sale often presents problematic practical considerations in terms of the time, cost, and feasibility involved in transferring title in the individual assets
  - This is particularly true for companies with a diverse group of assets, including various licenses and contracts, in multiple geographies
  - In a stock sale, by contrast, title to all the target's assets is transferred indirectly through the transfer of stock to the new owners

Deal Structure

Stock Deals Treated as Asset Deals for Tax Purposes

Section 338 Election

- In accordance with Section 338 of the Internal Revenue Code, an acquirer may choose to treat the purchase of the target's stock as an asset sale for tax purposes
- Enables the acquirer to write up the assets to their fair market value and receive the tax benefits associated with the depreciation and amortization of the asset step-up
- The acquirer typically assumes the additional tax burden associated with the deemed sale of the target's assets

338(h)(10) Election

- More common derivation of the 338 election is the joint 338(h)(10) election
- As with an asset sale, this structure is commonly used when the target is a subsidiary of a parent corporation
- 338(h)(10) election provides all the buyer tax benefits of an asset sale but without the practical issues around the transfer of individual asset titles
- Properly structured, the 338(h)(10) election creates an optimal outcome for both buyer and seller. Buyer is willing to pay the seller a higher price in return for acquiescing to a 338(h)(10) election
  - Affords tax benefits to the buyer from the asset step-up that results in the creation of tax-deductible depreciation and amortization
  - Results in a lower after-tax cost for the acquirer and greater after-tax proceeds for the seller

Buy-Side Valuation

- Valuation analysis is central to framing the acquirer's view on purchase price
  - Primary methodologies used to value a company—namely, comparable companies, precedent transactions, DCF, and LBO analysis—form the basis for this exercise
- Results of analyses are typically displayed on a graphic known as a "football field"
- Comprehensive buy-side M&A valuation analysis also typically includes analysis at various prices (AVP) and contribution analysis (typically used in stock-for-stock deals)
  - AVP, also known as a valuation matrix, displays the implied multiples paid at a range of transaction values and offer prices (for public targets) at set intervals
  - Contribution analysis examines the financial "contributions" made by acquirer and target to the pro forma entity prior to any transaction adjustments

Buy-Side Valuation

Football Field

- "Football field" is a commonly used visual aid for displaying the valuation ranges derived from the various methodologies
- For public companies, the football field also typically includes the target's 52-week trading range, along with a premiums paid range in line with precedent transactions in the given sector (e.g., 25%–40%)
  - May also reference the valuation implied by a range of target prices from equity research reports
- Used to help fine-tune the final valuation range, typically by analyzing the overlap of the multiple valuation methodologies
  - Certain methodologies receive greater emphasis depending on the situation
  - Valuation range is tested and analyzed within the context of merger consequences analysis to determine the ultimate bid price

Buy-Side Valuation

Football Field (continued) – Below is an illustrative football field for ValueCo; the diagonal line-shaded bar represents the present value of potential synergies

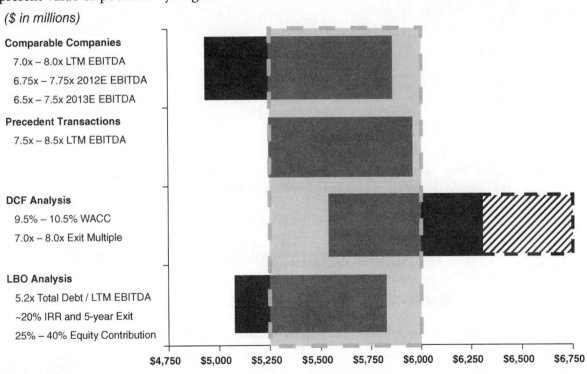

($ in millions)

Comparable Companies
7.0x – 8.0x LTM EBITDA
6.75x – 7.75x 2012E EBITDA
6.5x – 7.5x 2013E EBITDA

Precedent Transactions
7.5x – 8.5x LTM EBITDA

DCF Analysis
9.5% – 10.5% WACC
7.0x – 8.0x Exit Multiple

LBO Analysis
5.2x Total Debt / LTM EBITDA
~20% IRR and 5-year Exit
25% – 40% Equity Contribution

$4,750 $5,000 $5,250 $5,500 $5,750 $6,000 $6,250 $6,500 $6,750

Buy-Side Valuation

Analysis at Various Prices – Buy-side M&A valuation analysis employs analysis at various prices (AVP) to analyze and frame valuation

		Premium to Current Stock Price				
	Current	25%	30%	35%	40%	45%
Implied Offer Price per Share	$43.50	$54.38	$56.55	$58.73	$60.90	$63.08
Fully Diluted Shares Outstanding	79.7	79.9	80.0	80.0	80.1	80.1
Implied Offer Value	$3,468	$4,347	$4,523	$4,700	$4,877	$5,053
Plus: Total Debt	1,500	1,500	1,500	1,500	1,500	1,500
Less: Cash and Cash Equivalents	(250)	(250)	(250)	(250)	(250)	(250)
Implied Transaction Value	$4,718	$5,597	$5,773	$5,950	$6,127	$6,303

		Valuation Multiples						
Implied Transaction Value Multiples								
Sales	Metrics							BuyerCo
LTM	$3,385	1.4x	1.7x	1.7x	1.8x	1.8x	1.9x	1.8x
2012E	3,450	1.4x	1.6x	1.7x	1.7x	1.8x	1.8x	1.7x
2013E	3,709	1.3x	1.5x	1.6x	1.6x	1.7x	1.7x	1.6x
EBITDA								
LTM	$700	6.7x	8.0x	8.2x	8.5x	8.8x	9.0x	8.0x
2012E	725	6.5x	7.7x	8.0x	8.2x	8.5x	8.7x	7.8x
2013E	779	6.1x	7.2x	7.4x	7.6x	7.9x	8.1x	7.3x
EBIT								
LTM	$500	9.4x	11.2x	11.5x	11.9x	12.3x	12.6x	9.1x
2012E	518	9.1x	10.8x	11.1x	11.5x	11.8x	12.2x	8.8x
2013E	557	8.5x	10.1x	10.4x	10.7x	11.0x	11.3x	8.2x
Implied Offer Price Multiples								
EPS	Metrics							
LTM	$3.22	13.5x	16.9x	17.6x	18.2x	18.9x	19.6x	13.9x
2012E	3.36	12.9x	16.2x	16.8x	17.5x	18.1x	18.8x	13.5x
2013E	3.71	11.7x	14.6x	15.2x	15.8x	16.4x	17.0x	12.5x

Buy-Side Valuation

Contribution Analysis – Contribution Analysis depicts the financial "contributions" that each party makes to the pro forma entity in terms of sales, EBITDA, EBIT, net income, and equity value, typically expressed as a percentage

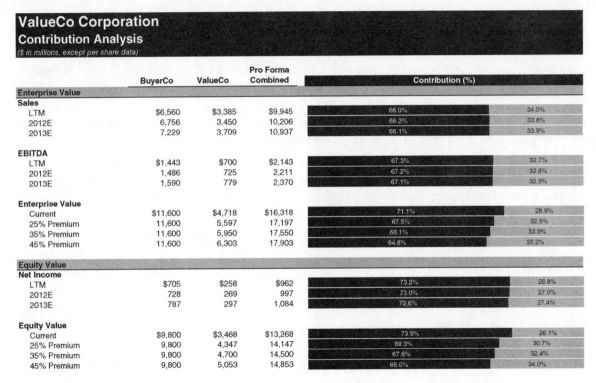

ValueCo Corporation
Contribution Analysis
($ in millions, except per share data)

	BuyerCo	ValueCo	Pro Forma Combined	Contribution (%)	
Enterprise Value					
Sales					
LTM	$6,560	$3,385	$9,945	66.0%	34.0%
2012E	6,756	3,450	10,206	66.2%	33.8%
2013E	7,229	3,709	10,937	66.1%	33.9%
EBITDA					
LTM	$1,443	$700	$2,143	67.3%	32.7%
2012E	1,486	725	2,211	67.2%	32.8%
2013E	1,590	779	2,370	67.1%	32.9%
Enterprise Value					
Current	$11,600	$4,718	$16,318	71.1%	28.9%
25% Premium	11,600	5,597	17,197	67.5%	32.5%
35% Premium	11,600	5,950	17,550	66.1%	33.9%
45% Premium	11,600	6,303	17,903	64.8%	35.2%
Equity Value					
Net Income					
LTM	$705	$258	$962	73.2%	26.8%
2012E	728	269	997	73.0%	27.0%
2013E	787	297	1,084	72.6%	27.4%
Equity Value					
Current	$9,800	$3,468	$13,268	73.9%	26.1%
25% Premium	9,800	4,347	14,147	69.3%	30.7%
35% Premium	9,800	4,700	14,500	67.6%	32.4%
45% Premium	9,800	5,053	14,853	66.0%	34.0%

Merger Consequences Analysis

- Merger consequences analysis measures the impact on EPS in the form of accretion/(dilution) analysis, as well as credit statistics through balance sheet effects
- Enables strategic buyers to fine-tune the ultimate purchase price, financing mix, and deal structure
- Requires key assumptions regarding purchase price and target company financials, as well as form of financing and deal structure
- For merger consequences analysis, first construct standalone operating models (income statement, balance sheet, and cash flow statement) for both the target and acquirer
  - These models are then combined into one pro forma financial model that incorporates various transaction-related adjustments
- The next slide displays the key merger consequences analysis outputs as linked from the merger model
  - Outputs include purchase price assumptions, sources and uses of funds, premium paid and exchange ratio, summary financial data, pro forma capitalization and credit statistics, accretion/(dilution) analysis, and implied acquisition multiples
  - Format allows the deal team to quickly review and spot-check the analysis and make adjustments to purchase price, financing mix, operating assumptions, and other key inputs as necessary

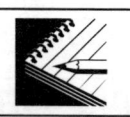

Merger Consequences Analysis

BuyerCo Acquisition of ValueCo
Merger Consequences Analysis
($ in millions, fiscal year ending December 31)

Financing Structure: Structure 1
Operating Scenario: Base

Transaction Summary

Sources of Funds

	Amount	% of Total Sources	Multiple of Pro Forma EBITDA 2012	Cumulative	Pricing
Revolving Credit Facility	-	- %	- x	- x	L+350 bps
Term Loan A	-	- %	- x	- x	NA
Term Loan B	2,200.0	34.6%	1.0x	1.0x	L+375 bps
Term Loan C	-	- %	- x	1.0x	NA
2nd Lien	-	- %	- x	1.0x	NA
Senior Notes	1,500.0	23.6%	0.6x	1.6x	7.500%
Senior Subordinated Notes	-	- %	- x	1.6x	NA
Issuance of Common Stock	2,350.0	37.0%	1.0x	2.6x	
Cash on Hand	300.0	4.7%	0.1x	2.7x	
Other	-	- %	- x	2.6x	
Total Sources	**$6,350.0**	**100.0%**	**2.7x**	**2.7x**	

Uses of Funds

	Amount	% of Total Uses
Purchase ValueCo Equity	$4,700.0	74.0%
Repay Existing Debt	1,500.0	23.6%
Tender / Call Premiums	20.0	0.3%
Transaction Fees	40.0	0.6%
Debt Financing Fees	90.0	1.4%
Total Uses	**$6,350.0**	**100.0%**

Premium Paid & Exchange Ratio

ValueCo Current Share Price	$43.50
Offer Price per Share	$58.73
Premium Paid	35%
BuyerCo Current Share Price	$70.00
Exchange Ratio	0.8x

Purchase Price

Offer Price per Share	$58.73
Fully Diluted Shares	80.0
Equity Purchase Price	$4,700.0
Plus: Existing Net Debt	1,250.0
Enterprise Value	$5,950.0

Acquisition Structure & Synergies

Stock Consideration for Equity	50%
Transaction Debt Raised	$3,700.0
% of ValueCo Enterprise Value	62%
Acquisition Type	Stock Sale
Year 1 Synergies	$100

Options

Financing Structure	1
Operating Scenario	1
Cash Flow Sweep	1
Cash Balance	1
Average Interest	1
Financing Fees	1

Pro Forma Combined Financial Summary

	Pro Forma 2012	1 2013	2 2014	3 2015	4 2016	5 2017
Sales	$10,205.8	$10,937.5	$11,593.7	$12,173.4	$12,660.3	$13,040.1
% growth	8.2%	7.2%	6.0%	5.0%	4.0%	3.0%
Gross Profit	$3,947.2	$4,230.4	$4,484.2	$4,708.4	$4,896.8	$5,043.7
% margin	38.7%	38.7%	38.7%	38.7%	38.7%	38.7%
EBITDA	$2,311.3	$2,469.7	$2,611.9	$2,737.5	$2,843.0	$2,925.3
% margin	22.6%	22.6%	22.5%	22.5%	22.5%	22.4%
Interest Expense	374.8	348.6	298.3	270.3	270.3	270.3
Net Income	$945.8	$1,043.3	$1,146.7	$1,231.4	$1,289.5	$1,336.0
% margin	9.3%	9.5%	9.9%	10.1%	10.2%	10.2%
Fully Diluted Shares	173.6	173.6	173.6	173.6	173.6	173.6
Diluted EPS	$5.45	$6.01	$6.62	$7.09	$7.43	$7.70
Cash Flow from Operating Activities		1,387.9	1,528.0	1,641.8	1,729.6	1,803.8
Less: Capital Expenditures		(383.6)	(406.3)	(427.1)	(444.2)	(457.5)
Free Cash Flow		$1,004.2	$1,121.2	$1,214.6	$1,285.4	$1,346.0
Senior Secured Debt	2,200.0	1,095.8	0.0	0.0	0.0	0.0
Senior Debt	5,900.0	4,795.8	3,700.0	3,700.0	3,700.0	3,700.0
Total Debt	5,900.0	4,795.8	3,700.0	3,700.0	3,700.0	3,700.0
Cash & Equivalents	350.0	250.0	275.4	1,490.0	2,775.4	4,121.5

Valuation Summary

	Target	Acquirer
Company Name	ValueCo	BuyerCo
Ticker	VLCO	BUY
Current Share Price (12/20/2012)	$43.50	$70.00
Premium to Current Share Price	35%	
Offer Price per Share	$58.73	
Fully Diluted Shares	80.0	140.0
Equity Value	$4,700.0	$9,800.0
Plus: Total Debt	1,500.0	2,200.0
Plus: Preferred Equity	-	-
Plus: Noncontrolling Interest	-	-
Less: Cash and Equivalents	(250.0)	(400.0)
Enterprise Value	$5,950.0	$11,600.0

Transaction Multiples

	Target Metric	Target Multiple	Acquirer Metric	Acquirer Multiple
Enterprise Value / LTM EBITDA	$700.0	8.5x	$1,443.1	8.0x
Enterprise Value / 2012E EBITDA	725.0	8.2x	1,496.3	7.8x
Enterprise Value / 2013E EBITDA	779.4	7.6x	1,590.3	7.3x
Equity Value / 2012E Net Income	$268.8	17.5x	$728.5	13.5x
Equity Value / 2013E Net Income	297.0	15.8x	786.6	12.5x

Pro Forma Ownership

	Shares	Ownership
Existing BuyerCo Shareholders	140.0	80.7%
Former ValueCo Shareholders	33.6	19.3%
Pro Forma Fully Diluted Shares	173.6	100.0%

Credit Statistics

	BuyerCo 2012	Pro Forma 2012	1 2013	2 2014	3 2015	4 2016	5 2017
EBITDA / Interest Expense	10.3x	6.2x	7.1x	8.8x	10.1x	10.5x	10.8x
(EBITDA - Capex) / Interest Expense	8.9x	5.2x	6.0x	7.4x	8.5x	8.9x	9.1x
Senior Secured Debt / EBITDA	- x	1.0x	0.4x	- x	- x	- x	- x
Senior Debt / EBITDA	1.5x	2.6x	1.9x	1.4x	1.4x	1.3x	1.3x
Total Debt / EBITDA	1.5x	2.6x	1.9x	1.4x	1.4x	1.3x	1.3x
Net Debt / EBITDA	1.2x	2.4x	1.8x	1.3x	0.8x	0.3x	(0.1x)
Debt / Total Capitalization	47.0%	55.3%	45.2%	34.7%	31.1%	28.1%	25.5%

Accretion / (Dilution) Analysis

BuyerCo Standalone Diluted EPS	$5.20	$5.62	$6.01	$6.36	$6.66	$6.89
ValueCo Standalone Diluted EPS	$3.36	$3.71	$4.08	$4.44	$4.70	$4.86
Pro Forma Combined Diluted EPS	$5.45	$6.01	$6.62	$7.09	$7.43	$7.70
Accretion / (Dilution) - $	$0.25	$0.39	$0.61	$0.74	$0.77	$0.81
Accretion / (Dilution) - %	4.7%	7.0%	10.1%	11.6%	11.5%	11.7%
Accretive / Dilutive	Accretive	Accretive	Accretive	Accretive	Accretive	Accretive
Breakeven Pre-Tax Synergies / (Cushion)	($66)	($105)	($170)	($206)	($217)	($225)

Annual EPS Accretion / (Dilution) Sensitivity Analysis - Premium Paid

Offer Price	Premium	2012	2013	2014	2015	2016
$54.38	25%	7.3%	9.5%	12.4%	13.6%	13.7%
$56.55	30%	6.0%	8.2%	11.2%	12.6%	12.6%
$58.73	35%	4.7%	7.0%	10.1%	11.6%	11.6%
$60.90	40%	3.5%	5.7%	8.9%	10.5%	10.6%
$63.08	45%	2.2%	4.5%	7.7%	9.4%	9.7%

2013E EPS Accretion / (Dilution) Sensitivity Analysis - Premium Paid & Consideration Mix

		% Stock Consideration Mix				
Offer Price	Premium	0%	25%	50%	75%	100%
$54.38	25%	25.0%	16.5%	9.5%	6.4%	1.3%
$56.55	30%	24.1%	15.3%	8.2%	5.0%	(0.1%)
$58.73	35%	23.2%	14.2%	7.0%	3.7%	(1.5%)
$60.90	40%	22.2%	13.1%	5.7%	2.4%	(2.9%)
$63.08	45%	21.3%	11.9%	4.5%	1.1%	(4.2%)

Merger Consequences Analysis

Purchase Price Assumptions

- Assume BuyerCo is offering $58.73 for each share of ValueCo common stock
  - Represents a 35% premium to the company's current share price of $43.50
- A $58.73 offer price with fully diluted shares outstanding of approximately 80 million for ValueCo implies an equity purchase price of $4,700 million
  - Adding net debt of $1,250 million equates to an enterprise value of $5,950 million, or 8.5x LTM EBITDA
- EBITDA purchase price multiple is 0.5x higher than the 8.0x LTM EBITDA multiple under the LBO scenario shown in Chapter 5
- BuyerCo is able to pay higher price due to its ability to extract $100 million in annual synergies from combination
  - On a synergy-adjusted basis, BuyerCo is only paying 7.4x LTM EBITDA for ValueCo

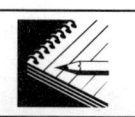

Merger Consequences Analysis

($ in millions, except per share data)

Purchase Price Assumptions			
		Multiple	
	Amount	**w/o Synergies**	**w/Synergies**
ValueCo Current Share Price	$43.50		
Premium to Current Share Price	35%		
Offer Price per Share	**$58.73**	**18.2x**	**14.7x**
Fully Diluted Shares Outstanding	80.0		
Equity Purchase Price	**$4,700.0**		
Plus: Total Debt	1,500.0		
Less: Cash and Cash Equivalents	(250.0)		
Enterprise Value	**$5,950.0**	**8.5x**	**7.4x**
LTM EPS		$3.22	$4.00
LTM EBITDA		$700.0	$800.0

Merger Consequences Analysis

Purchase Price Assumptions (continued)

Sources of Funds

- Assume a 50% stock / 50% cash consideration offered to ValueCo shareholders
- $2,350 million of stock (50% of $4,700 billion equity purchase price for ValueCo), or 33.6 million shares ($2,350 billion / BuyerCo share price of $70.00)
- $2,200 million of term loan B
- $1,500 million of senior notes
- $300 million of cash on hand (including $50 million of existing BuyerCo cash)

Uses of Funds

- Purchase of ValueCo's equity for $4,700 million
- Repayment of ValueCo's existing $1,000 million term loan and $500 million senior notes
- Payment of total fees and expenses of $150 million, consisting of: i) M&A advisory and other transaction fees of $40 million, ii) debt financing fees of $90 million, and iii) tender/call premiums of $20 million

Merger Consequences Analysis

Purchase Price Assumptions (continued)

($ in millions)

Sources of Funds					
		% of Total	**Multiple of Pro Forma EBITDA**		
	Amount	**Sources**	**2012**	**Cumulative**	**Pricing**
Revolving Credit Facility[a]	-	- %	- x	- x	L+350 bps
Term Loan A	-	- %	- x	- x	NA
Term Loan B[a]	2,200.0	34.6%	1.0x	1.0x	L+375 bps
Term Loan C	-	- %	- x	1.0x	NA
2nd Lien	-	- %	- x	1.0x	NA
Senior Notes	1,500.0	23.6%	0.6x	1.6x	7.500%
Senior Subordinated Notes	-	- %	- x	1.6x	NA
Issuance of Common Stock	2,350.0	37.0%	1.0x	2.6x	
Cash on Hand	300.0	4.7%	0.1x	2.7x	
Other	-	- %	- x	2.6x	
Total Sources	**$6,350.0**	**100.0%**	**2.7x**	**2.7x**	

Uses of Funds		
		% of Total
	Amount	**Uses**
Purchase ValueCo Equity	$4,700.0	74.0%
Repay Existing Debt	1,500.0	23.6%
Tender / Call Premiums	20.0	0.3%
Debt Financing Fees	90.0	1.4%
Transaction Fees	40.0	0.6%
Total Uses	**$6,350.0**	**100.0%**

[a] Revolver size of $500 million. Revolver and term loan B coupons include 1% LIBOR floor.

Merger Consequences Analysis

Goodwill Created

- Once the sources and uses of funds are inputted into the model, goodwill is calculated
  - For the purchase of ValueCo by BuyerCo, there are additional complexities in calculating goodwill versus LBO Analysis
  - Assume a write-up of the target's tangible and intangible assets, as well as a deferred tax liability (DTL)
- Goodwill is calculated by first subtracting ValueCo's net identifiable assets of $2,500 million ($3,500 million shareholders' equity – $1,000 million existing goodwill) from the equity purchase price of $4,700 million, which results in an allocable purchase price premium of $2,200 million
- Next, subtract the combined write-ups of ValueCo's tangible and intangible assets of $550 million from the allocable purchase price premium (based on a 15% write-up for the tangible assets and a 10% write-up for the intangible assets)
- Given this is a stock deal, then add the DTL of $209 million, which is calculated as the sum of the asset write-ups multiplied by BuyerCo's marginal tax rate of 38%

Merger Consequences Analysis

= - (Allocable Purchase Price Premium × Assumed Tangible Asset Write-Up)
= - ($2,200 million × 15%)

= - (ValueCo Shareholders' Equity - Existing Goodwill)
= - ($3,500 million - $1,000 million)

($ in millions)

Goodwill Calculation	Allocation %	
Equity Purchase Price		$4,700.0
Less: ValueCo Net Identifiable Assets		(2,500.0)
Total Allocable Purchase Premium		**$2,200.0**
Less: Tangible Asset Write-Up	15%	(330.0)
Less: Intangible Asset Write-Up	10%	(220.0)
Plus: Deferred Tax Liability		$209.0
Goodwill Created in Transaction		**$1,859.0**

= - (Assumed Tangible Asset Write-Up + Assumed Intangible Asset Write-Up)
  × BuyerCo Marginal Tax Rate
= - (-$330 million + -$220 million) × 38%

= - (Allocable Purchase Price Premium × Assumed Intangible Asset Write-Up)
= - ($2,200 million × 10%)

Merger Consequences Analysis

Goodwill Created (continued)

Annual Depreciation & Amortization from Write-Ups

- Assumed write-ups of ValueCo's tangible and intangible assets are linked to the adjustments columns in the balance sheet and increase the value of PP&E and intangible assets, respectively
- Additions to the balance sheet are amortized over a defined period
  - Assume 15 years for both the tangible and intangible write-ups
- Creates additional annual PP&E depreciation and intangible amortization of $22 million and $14.7 million, respectively

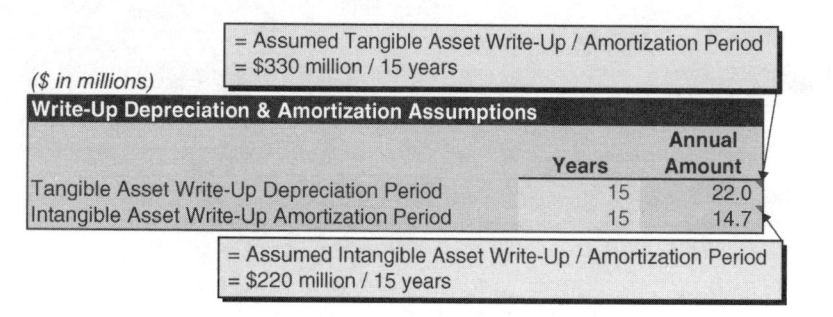

($ in millions)

= Assumed Tangible Asset Write-Up / Amortization Period
= $330 million / 15 years

Write-Up Depreciation & Amortization Assumptions	Years	Annual Amount
Tangible Asset Write-Up Depreciation Period	15	22.0
Intangible Asset Write-Up Amortization Period	15	14.7

= Assumed Intangible Asset Write-Up / Amortization Period
= $220 million / 15 years

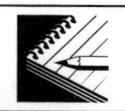

Merger Consequences Analysis

Balance Sheet Effects

- Balance sheet considerations play an important role in merger consequences analysis, factoring into both purchase price and financing structure considerations
  - Must be carefully analyzed in conjunction with EPS accretion/(dilution)
- Most accretive financing structure (typically all debt) may not be the most attractive or viable from a balance sheet or credit perspective
  - As such, the optimal financing structure must strike the proper balance between cost of capital (and corresponding earnings impact) and pro forma credit profile
- As in the LBO model, once the sources and uses of funds are finalized and goodwill created is calculated, each amount is linked to the appropriate cell in the adjustments columns adjacent to the opening balance sheet
  - These adjustments, combined with the sum of the acquirer and target balance sheet items, serve to bridge the opening balance sheet to the pro forma closing balance sheet
  - After adjustments are made, calculate the pro forma credit statistics and compare them to the pre-transaction standalone metrics

Merger Consequences Analysis

Balance Sheet Effects (continued)

Credit Statistics

- Most widely used credit statistics are grouped into leverage ratios (e.g., debt-to-EBITDA and debt-to-total-capitalization) and coverage ratios (e.g., EBITDA-to-interest-expense)
  - Rating agencies tend to establish target ratio thresholds for companies that correspond to given ratings categories
  - Acquirers are often guided by the desire to maintain key target ratios in crafting their M&A financing structure
- As shown on the next slide, assuming a 50% stock/50% cash consideration offered to ValueCo shareholders, BuyerCo's credit statistics weaken slightly given the incremental debt raise
  - Pro forma for the deal, BuyerCo's debt-to-EBITDA increases from 1.5x to 2.6x while debt-to-total-capitalization of 47% increases to 55.3%
  - By the end of 2013E, however, pro forma entity deleverages to below 2.0x and further decreases to 1.4x by the end of 2014E (in line with BuyerCo's pre-transaction leverage)
  - By the end of 2013E, debt-to-total capitalization reaches 45.2%, which is slightly lower than the pre-transaction level
  - EBITDA-to-interest-expense decreases from 10.3x pre-deal to 7.1x by the end of 2013E while capex-adjusted coverage decreases from 8.9x to 6.0x
  - Coverage ratios return to roughly pre-transaction levels by the end of 2015E

Merger Consequences Analysis

($ in millions, fiscal year ending December 31)

Capitalization

	BuyerCo 2012	ValueCo 2012	Adjustments +	Adjustments −	Pro forma 2012	1 2013	2 2014	3 2015	4 2016	5 2017
							Projection Period			
Cash	$400.0	$250.0		(300.0)	$350.0	$250.0	$275.4	$1,490.0	$2,775.4	$4,121.5
Revolving Credit Facility	-	-			-	-	-	-	-	-
ValueCo Term Loan	-	1,000.0		(1,000.0)	-	-	-	-	-	-
New Term Loan B	-	-	2,200.0		2,200.0	1,095.8	-	-	-	-
Other Debt	-	-			-	-	-	-	-	-
Total Senior Secured Debt	-	$1,000.0			$2,200.0	$1,095.8	-	-	-	-
BuyerCo Senior Notes	2,200.0	-			2,200.0	2,200.0	2,200.0	2,200.0	2,200.0	2,200.0
ValueCo Senior Notes	-	500.0		(500.0)	-	-	-	-	-	-
New Senior Notes	-	-	1,500.0		1,500.0	1,500.0	1,500.0	1,500.0	1,500.0	1,500.0
Total Senior Debt	$2,200.0	$1,500.0			$5,900.0	$4,795.8	$3,700.0	$3,700.0	$3,700.0	$3,700.0
Senior Subordinated Notes	-	-			-	-	-	-	-	-
Total Debt	$2,200.0	$1,500.0			$5,900.0	$4,795.8	$3,700.0	$3,700.0	$3,700.0	$3,700.0
Shareholders' Equity	2,480.0	3,500.0	2,290.0	(3,500.0)	4,770.0	5,813.3	6,962.0	8,193.4	9,482.9	10,818.9
Total Capitalization	$4,680.0	$5,000.0			$10,670.0	$10,609.1	$10,662.0	$11,893.4	$13,182.9	$14,518.9
% of Bank Debt Repaid					-	50.2%	100.0%	100.0%	100.0%	100.0%

Credit Statistics

	BuyerCo 2012	ValueCo 2012	Adjustments	Pro forma 2012	1 2013	2 2014	3 2015	4 2016	5 2017
EBITDA	$1,486.3	$725.0	100.0	$2,311.3	$2,469.7	$2,611.9	$2,737.5	$2,843.0	$2,925.3
Capital Expenditures	202.7	155.3		357.9	383.8	406.8	427.1	444.2	457.5
Interest Expense	144.4	85.9	144.5	374.8	348.6	296.3	270.3	270.3	270.3
EBITDA / Interest Expense	10.3x	8.4x		6.2x	7.1x	8.8x	10.1x	10.5x	10.8x
(EBITDA - Capex) / Interest Expense	8.9x	6.6x		5.2x	6.0x	7.4x	8.5x	8.9x	9.1x
Senior Secured Debt / EBITDA	- x	1.4x		1.0x	0.4x	- x	- x	- x	- x
Senior Debt / EBITDA	1.5x	2.1x		2.6x	1.9x	1.4x	1.4x	1.3x	1.3x
Total Debt / EBITDA	1.5x	2.1x		2.6x	1.9x	1.4x	1.4x	1.3x	1.3x
Net Debt / EBITDA	1.2x	1.7x		2.4x	1.8x	1.3x	0.8x	0.3x	(0.1x)
% Debt / Total Capitalization	47.0%	30.0%		55.3%	45.2%	34.7%	31.1%	28.1%	25.5%

Debt / EBITDA

Premium Paid	% Stock Consideration Mix 0%	25%	50%	75%	100%
25%	3.4x	3.0x	2.5x	2.0x	1.5x
30%	3.5x	3.0x	2.5x	2.0x	1.5x
35%	3.6x	3.1x	2.6x	2.0x	1.5x
40%	3.7x	3.1x	2.6x	2.0x	1.5x
45%	3.7x	3.2x	2.6x	2.1x	1.5x

EBITDA / Interest Expense

Premium Paid	% Stock Consideration Mix 0%	25%	50%	75%	100%
25%	4.9x	5.5x	6.3x	8.7x	11.0x
30%	4.8x	5.4x	6.2x	8.6x	11.0x
35%	4.7x	5.3x	6.2x	8.6x	11.0x
40%	4.6x	5.2x	6.1x	8.5x	11.0x
45%	4.5x	5.2x	6.0x	8.4x	11.0x

Merger Consequences Analysis

Accretion/(Dilution) Analysis

- Accretion/(dilution) analysis measures the effects of a transaction on a potential acquirer's earnings, assuming a given financing structure
  - Centers on comparing the acquirer's earnings per share (EPS) pro forma for the transaction versus on a standalone basis
- If the pro forma combined EPS is lower than the acquirer's standalone EPS, the transaction is said to be *dilutive*; conversely, if the pro forma EPS is higher, the transaction is said to be *accretive*
- A rule of thumb for 100% stock transactions is that when an acquirer purchases a target with a lower P/E, the acquisition is accretive
  - Concept is intuitive—when a company pays a lower multiple for the target's earnings than the multiple at which its own earnings trade, the transaction is de facto accretive
- Transactions where an acquirer purchases a higher P/E target are de facto dilutive
  - Sizable synergies, however, may serve to offset this financial convention and result in such acquisitions being accretive
  - Transaction-related expenses such as depreciation and amortization, on the other hand, have the opposite effect
- Acquirers target accretive transactions as they create value for their shareholders due to the fact that the market usually responds favorably

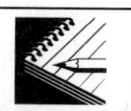

Merger Consequences Analysis

Accretion/(Dilution) Analysis (continued)

- Accretion/(dilution) analysis is usually a key screening mechanism for potential acquirers
  - Acquirers do not pursue transactions that are dilutive over the foreseeable earnings projection period due to the potential destructive effects on shareholder value
  - May be exceptions in certain situations
- Key drivers for accretion/(dilution) are purchase price, acquirer and target projected earnings, synergies, and form of financing, most notably the debt/equity mix and cost of debt
  - Calculations must also reflect transaction-related effects pertaining to deal structure, such as the write-up of tangible and intangible assets
  - Maximum accretive effects are served by negotiating as low a purchase price as possible, sourcing the cheapest form of financing, choosing the optimal deal structure, and identifying significant achievable synergies
- Transaction expenses related to M&A advisory and financing fees may also be factored into accretion/(dilution) analysis
  - M&A advisory fees are typically expensed upfront while debt financing fees are amortized over the life of the security
  - In many cases, however, transaction fees are treated as non-recurring items and excluded from accretion/(dilution) analysis, which is the approach we adopt in our analysis

---

Merger Consequences Analysis

Accretion/(Dilution) Analysis Steps

- Step I. Enter the acquirer's standalone projected operating income (EBIT)
- Step II. Add the target's standalone projected operating income (EBIT)
- Step III. Add expected synergies from the transaction for the projection period
- Step IV. Subtract transaction-related depreciation and amortization expenses (typically associated with writing up the target's tangible and intangible assets)
- Step V. Subtract the acquirer's existing interest expense
- Step VI. Subtract the incremental interest expense associated with the new transaction debt to calculate pro forma earnings before taxes
- Step VII. Subtract the tax expense at the acquirer's tax rate to arrive at pro forma combined net income
- Step VIII. In the event stock is used as a portion, or all, of the purchase price, add the new shares issued as part of the transaction to the acquirer's existing fully diluted shares outstanding
- Step IX. Divide pro forma net income by the pro forma fully diluted shares outstanding to arrive at pro forma combined EPS
- Step X. Compare pro forma EPS with the acquirer's standalone EPS to determine whether the transaction is accretive or dilutive

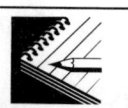

Merger Consequences Analysis

Accretion/(Dilution) Analysis – Below is a graphical depiction of the accretion/(dilution) calculation

Merger Consequences Analysis

($ in millions, except per share data)

Accretion / (Dilution) Analysis - 50% Stock / 50% Cash

	Pro forma 2012	1 2013	2 2014	3 2015	4 2016	5 2017
				Projection Period		
BuyerCo EBIT		$1,317.4	$1,409.6	$1,494.2	$1,568.9	$1,631.6	$1,680.6
ValueCo EBIT		518.0	556.9	590.3	619.8	644.6	663.9
Synergies		100.0	100.0	100.0	100.0	100.0	100.0
Pro Forma Combined EBIT (pre-deal structure)		$1,935.4	$2,066.4	$2,184.4	$2,288.7	$2,376.2	$2,444.5
Depreciation from Write-Up		22.0	22.0	22.0	22.0	22.0	22.0
Amortization from Write-Up		14.7	14.7	14.7	14.7	14.7	14.7
Pro Forma Combined EBIT		$1,898.7	$2,029.8	$2,147.8	$2,252.0	$2,339.5	$2,407.8
Standalone Net Interest Expense		142.4	140.6	137.0	133.0	128.9	124.5
Incremental Net Interest Expense		230.9	206.4	158.0	132.8	130.8	128.6
Earnings Before Taxes		$1,525.4	$1,682.7	$1,852.8	$1,986.1	$2,079.9	$2,154.8
Income Tax Expense @ 38.0%		579.7	639.4	704.0	754.7	790.4	818.8
Pro Forma Combined Net Income		$945.8	$1,043.3	$1,148.7	$1,231.4	$1,289.5	$1,336.0
BuyerCo Standalone Net Income		$728.5	$786.8	$841.5	$890.2	$931.7	$964.8
Standalone Fully Diluted Shares Outstanding		140.0	140.0	140.0	140.0	140.0	140.0
Net New Shares Issued in Transaction		33.6	33.6	33.6	33.6	33.6	33.6
Pro Forma Fully Diluted Shares Outstanding		173.6	173.6	173.6	173.6	173.6	173.6
Pro Forma Combined Diluted EPS		$5.45	$6.01	$6.62	$7.09	$7.43	$7.70
BuyerCo Standalone Diluted EPS		5.20	5.62	6.01	6.36	6.66	6.89
Accretion / (Dilution) - $		$0.25	$0.39	$0.61	$0.74	$0.77	$0.81
Accretion / (Dilution) - %		4.7%	7.0%	10.1%	11.6%	11.6%	11.7%
Accretive / Dilutive		Accretive	Accretive	Accretive	Accretive	Accretive	Accretive
Included Pre-Tax Synergies		$100.0	$100.0	$100.0	$100.0	$100.0	$100.0
Additional Pre-Tax Synergies to Breakeven		(68.7)	(109.5)	(170.1)	(205.9)	(216.8)	(225.5)
Required Synergies to Breakeven / (Cushion)		$31.3	($9.5)	($70.1)	($105.9)	($116.8)	($125.5)

Annual EPS Accretion / (Dilution) Sensitivity Analysis - Premium Paid

Offer Price	Premium	Year				
		2012	2013	2014	2015	2016
$54.38	25%	7.3%	9.5%	12.4%	13.6%	13.7%
$56.55	30%	6.0%	8.2%	11.2%	12.6%	12.6%
$58.73	35%	4.7%	7.0%	10.1%	11.6%	11.6%
$60.90	40%	3.5%	5.7%	8.9%	10.5%	10.6%
$63.08	45%	2.2%	4.5%	7.7%	9.4%	9.7%

2012E EPS Accretion / (Dilution) Sensitivity Analysis - Premium Paid & Consideration Mix

Offer Price	Premium	% Stock Consideration Mix				
		0%	25%	50%	75%	100%
$54.38	25%	25.0%	16.5%	9.5%	6.4%	1.3%
$56.55	30%	24.1%	15.3%	8.2%	5.0%	(0.1%)
$58.73	35%	23.2%	14.2%	7.0%	3.7%	(1.5%)
$60.90	40%	22.2%	13.1%	5.7%	2.4%	(2.9%)
$63.08	45%	21.3%	11.9%	4.5%	1.1%	(4.2%)

Breakeven Synergies Sensitivity Analysis

Offer Price	Premium	Estimated Synergies				
		$0	$50	$100	$150	$200
$54.38	25%	2.9%	6.2%	9.5%	12.7%	16.0%
$56.55	30%	1.7%	5.0%	8.2%	11.5%	14.7%
$58.73	35%	0.5%	3.7%	7.0%	10.2%	13.4%
$60.90	40%	(0.7%)	2.5%	5.7%	8.9%	12.1%
$63.08	45%	(1.8%)	1.3%	4.5%	7.7%	10.9%

Breakeven Synergies Sensitivity Analysis

Offer Price	Premium	Pre-Tax Synergies Required to Breakeven				
		2012	2013	2014	2015	2016
$54.38	25%	($4)	($47)	($105)	($139)	($151)
$56.55	30%	$14	($28)	($88)	($122)	($134)
$58.73	35%	$31	($9)	($70)	($106)	($117)
$60.90	40%	$49	$9	($51)	($88)	($100)
$63.08	45%	$67	$28	($31)	($70)	($83)

Index

A

ability to pay, 249, 264
ABL facility. *See* asset based lending facility
accountants, 225
accounting, 154, 232, 266, 268
accounts payable, 89, 90
accounts receivable, 87
accretion/(dilution) analysis, 278, 290–294
accretive, 287, 290–292
accrued liabilities, 90
acquisition currency, 263
acquisition financing, 43, 46, 48, 260
adjustments
    balance sheet, 172
    management projections, 76, 160
    mid-year convention, 111
    non-recurring items, 24
    purchase price and financing structure, 161, 172, 198, 278, 286–287
    recent events, 24, 47
    year-end discounting, 110, 111
administrative agent, 183

administrative agent fee, 183
all-cash transaction, 45, 52
amortization,
    deferred financing fees, of, 161–162, 183, 291
    intangible assets, of, 83, 266
    schedule, for term loans (*See also* depreciation & amortization (D&A))
    term loan, 124, 180, 261
amortizing term loans, 124. *See also* term loan A
analysis at various prices (AVP), 273, 276
announcement,
    earnings, 8,
    transactions, 48, 51, 53, 59, 61–62, 240, 251
annual report. *See* Form 10-K
antitrust, 242
arranger, 123–124
asset base, 19, 131, 138
asset based lending (ABL) facility, 138
asset sale, 264, 270–272
auction, 45, 202, 205–208, 210, 212–213, 215, 219, 227, 230, 238, 246. *See also* broad auction; targeted auction
AVP. *See* analysis at various prices

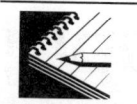

B

back-end short form merger, 244
balance sheet, 7, 84, 85, 156–157, 159, 161, 163, 166–167,
    172–174, 176, 185, 248, 249, 258–260, 266 268, 278,
    286–288
  in LBO analysis, 161, 163, 166, 172, 185–186
bank book, 125
bank debt, 123, 124, 131, 135, 136, 138, 139, 146–151, 180,
    189
bank lenders, 124, 144
bank meeting, 124
bankruptcy, 131
barriers to entry, 129, 131
Base Case, 76, 160
Base Rate, 138
basic shares outstanding, 7, 11
benchmarking analysis, 28, 49
  comparable companies analysis, 28–32
  precedent transactions analysis, 64–65
benchmark rate. *See* Base Rate; London Interbank Offered
    Rate (LIBOR)
Berkshire Hathaway, 258
beta, 99–103
beta ([beta]), 100–102

relevering, 102
  unlevering, 101
bidders. *See* prospective buyers
bidding strategy, 155
Bloomberg, 6–8
board approval, 236, 240
board of directors, 126, 221, 233, 238–240
bond investors, 125
book value, 83
borrower, 136, 138, 143, 144, 147–148, 261
bridge financing, 245
broad auction, 205–206, 210, 212
business disruption, 206, 210
business profile, 5, 64
buy-side advisory, 247–294

C

CA. *See* confidentiality agreement
CAGR. *See* compound annual growth rate
calendarization of financial data, 24
calendar year, 7, 24, 111
call premium, 282
call price, 147
call protection, 147

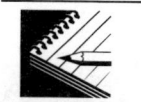

Q

quarterly report. *See* Form 10-Q

R

ranking, 27, 137
rating agencies, 6, 259, 288. *See also* Fitch Ratings, Moody's
and S&P
Ratios, 2, 9–26, 28, 40, 49–63
Ratio Test, 149
redemptions, 147
refinancing, 58, 154
registration statement, 47, 48
regulatory approvals, 207, 233, 242
reporting period, 73
representations and warranties, 234
restructurings, 3, 41, 154
return on assets (ROA), 10, 19
return on equity (ROE), 10, 18
return on invested capital (ROIC), 10, 18
return on investment (ROI), 10, 18–19
revenues, 252, 253, 266, 272. *See also* sales
revolver availability, 245, 261
revolving credit facilities (revolver), 178
risk-free rate, 99, 100

ROA. *See* return on assets
roadshow, 125
ROE. *See* return on equity
ROI. *See* return on investment
ROIC. *See* return on invested capital
roll-up, 122

S

sale process, 4, 73, 158, 209–211, 239, 246
sales, 13
   projection of, 78–79
scale, 74, 129, 134, 263
Schedule 13E-3, 47
Schedule 14A. *See* proxy statement
Schedule 14D-9, 47
Schedule TO, 47
S Corp, 265
screening
   for comparable acquisitions, 6, 42
   for comparable companies, 6
SEC. *See* Securities and Exchange Commission
SEC filings, 4, 7, 8, 59, 73, 239
second round, of auction, 218, 228–235
section 338, 272

Focus on
Index

strike price. *See* exercise price
structural protections, 56
structural subordination, 145
subordination provisions, 144–145
sub-sector, 28
summary output sheets, 9, 49
suppliers, 73, 90, 225, 252, 254, 256
synergies, 41, 44–45, 47, 50, 59, 62–63, 135, 212, 246, 249, 251–255, 263, 275, 290–292
systematic risk, 99–101

T
tangible assets, 266, 284
tangible value, 62, 126, 258
targeted auction, 205, 206, 210
target management, 126, 128
taxable event, 52
tax basis, 268, 270–271
tax deductibility, 95, 133
tax expense, 13–14, 16, 183, 292
    projection of, 82
tax regime, 13–14, 16, 17, 25
T-bills, 100, 262
T-bonds, 100

teaser, 213–215, 217, 219
tender offers, 244
tenor. *See* maturity
term. *See* maturity
terminal value, 70–73, 91, 106–112, 117, 118
terminal year, 78, 106–108
termination provisions, 234
term loan A, 180
term loan B, 180, 282
term loan facilities, 180
time value of money, 109
T-notes, 100
total interest expense, 183
trading comps. *See* comparable companies analysis
trading multiples, 2, 7, 9–28, 33, 107, 111
trailing twelve months (TTM). *See* last twelve months
transaction comps. *See* precedent transactions analysis
transaction multiples, 40, 46, 49–63, 67
transaction structure, 156, 167–172, 234
transaction value, 58–59, 273
triggering event, 7
two-step tender process, 244